The Home Run Hitter's Guide to Fundraising

Happy About Raising Capital Without Pitching

By Dan Sapp

HappyAbout.info

21265 Stevens Creek Blvd.
Suite 205
Cupertino, CA 95014

The Home Run Hitter's Guide to Fundraising: Happy About Raising Capital Without Pitching

First Printing: July 2, 2007
Paperback ISBN: 1-60005-059-X
Place of Publication: Silicon Valley, California, USA
Library of Congress Number: 2007931798

eBook ISBN: 1-60005-060-3

Trademarks

Warning and Disclaimer

Praise for The Home Run Hitter's Guide to Fundraising (from the back cover)

"I can tell you from personal experience that the process outlined in 'The Home Run Hitter's Guide to Fundraising' will help any business person get results in any important business communication whether you are pitching venture capitalists or leading an important meeting. The ideas are powerful and the process works."
David Kennedy, Associate Dean for Development, Stanford University Graduate School of Business

"'The Home Run Hitter's Guide to Fundraising' and the Delta Communication Model are incredibly useful tools for entrepreneurs preparing to talk to investors. I know our portfolio companies have had a real advantage using this process as they have prepared for VC meetings. If you want your company to stand out in a sea of PowerPoint, put the information in this book to work."
Jennifer McFarlane, CEO Astia (Business Accelerator), San Francisco, CA

"We have used the ideas in this book to great success not only with sales people but also for executive level communication and international business partner communication. If getting results when you talk is important to you as a leader, then this book can be an incredibly useful resource."
Matt Davenport, VP Sales, Skyy Spirits, San Francisco, CA

Publisher

- Mitchell Levy, http://www.happyabout.info/

Executive Editor

- Elisabetta Ghisini

Cover Designer

- Cate Calson, http://www.calsongraphics.com/

Graphics by

- Panastream Multimedia, http://www.panastream.com

Dedication

This book is dedicated to the fearless entrepreneurs of the world who constantly inspire us with their imagination, dedication, and stamina. Without you, we would still be sending smoke signals and painting on cave walls. This book is also dedicated to the next generation of entrepreneurs who have both the power and the responsibility to heal a struggling planet, and make peace and progress sustainable and profitable.

Acknowledgements

I want to thank the people who helped make this book a much better reality than it could ever have been without them.

First, thanks to the O'Bryan boys at PanaStream. You are more than a production team, you are creative machines. With Yvonne's help, you not only helped me and my voice - you made it deeper, more resonant, and smarter than the original.

To Mitchell and Elisabetta at "Happy About", thanks for taking a chance and putting this in front of a larger audience. I look forward to the journey.

To my sister Carver, you brought more than a professional proofreader's eye to the project. The creativity, insights and courage it took to make incredibly useful suggestions to a sometimes crusty younger brother have made this a much cleaner and more useful product.

I especially want to thank my clients, from academia to investment services and from technology to the spirits industry, for giving me the faith to stick with the contrarian stand and trust my instincts. I deeply appreciate the help of the folks from venture capital and beyond who corrected some of my misconceptions about the industry and who shall forever remain nameless in order to protect their innocence.

I want to thank my dear friend, way-shower, fellow seeker and partner in crime, Charles. Whether reminding me to relax, grind, or "suck it up," you were always there and the path seemed straighter for the company.

Finally, to my wife Anne, I can never thank you enough for your patience, love, and support. My late nights, early mornings and even grumpier disposition than normal must have had you looking forward to the end of this thing at least as much as I have.

Thank you all,

Dan Sapp

A Message From Happy About®

Thank you for your purchase of this Happy About book. It is available online at http://happyabout.info/homerun-fundraising.php or at other online and physical bookstores.

- Please contact us for quantity discounts at sales@happyabout.info
- If you want to be informed by e-mail of upcoming Happy About® books, please e-mail bookupdate@happyabout.info

Happy About is interested in you if you are an author who would like to submit a non-fiction book proposal or a corporation that would like to have a book written for you. Please contact us by e-mail editorial@happyabout.info or phone (1-408-257-3000).

Other Happy About books available include:

- Moving From Vision to Reality http://happyabout.info/myfaith/vision2reality.php
- Climbing the Ladder of Business Inteligence: http://happyabout.info/climbing-ladder.php
- Overcoming Inventoritis: http://happyabout.info/overcoming-inventoritis.php
- Happy About People-to-People Lending With Prosper.com: http://happyabout.info/prosper/
- Happy About Online Networking: http://happyabout.info/onlinenetworking.php
- Happy About Apartment Management: http://happyabout.info/apartment-management.php
- Confessions of a Resilient Entrepreneur: http://happyabout.info/confessions-entrepreneur.php
- Memoirs of the Money Lady: http://happyabout.info/memoirs-money-lady.php
- 30-Day Bootcamp: Your Ultimate Life Makeover: http://happyabout.info/30daybootcamp/life-makeover.php
- The Business Rule Revolution: http://happyabout.info/business-rule-revolution.php
- Happy About Global Software Test Automation: http://happyabout.info/globalswtestautomation.php
- Happy About Joint Venturing: http://happyabout.info/jointventuring.php
- Happy About LinkedIn for Recruiting: http://happyabout.info/linkedin4recruiting.php
- Happy About Website Payments with PayPal http://happyabout.info/paypal.php

Contents

Foreword by Aaron Gershenberg, EVP for the Venture Group at Silicon Valley Bank

As an executive, every time you talk you have an opportunity to move your business forward. Whether you're raising venture capital, motivating the team or brainstorming for creative solutions to pressing business challenges, the leader who talks "on purpose" (strategically and with empathy) is the one who gets results throughout the organization. I've known Dan Sapp for ten years and have worked with him on my own communication development as well as seen the results of the work he has done with executives here. "The Home Run Hitter's Guide to Fundraising" is a compelling, effective, highly readable application of Dan's thinking process to a unique communication situation that can spell the early success or failure of a young company. If all of my executives and clients used this process, I'm convinced we would all spend a lot less time narrating and translating valueless PowerPoint slides and more time taking advantage of market opportunities.

With the days of the "Dot-Com" bubble beginning to fade from memory and with more and more venture capital back in the pipeline, smart MBA's from Stanford, MIT, and Harvard have worked their fingers to the bone developing companies that are fundable. They've turned over every rock they could to get meetings on Sand Hill Road and other centers of venture capital. The problem is that once they get those meetings many still want to turn off the lights, read from text-heavy PowerPoint slides, and put investors to sleep.

It is more than a waste of intellectual capability – it is a crime against commerce. Every time it happens, smart folks leave money on the table. You don't want to leave money on the table. You want money in your bank account. So, if you are ready to stretch your empathy muscles, connect and communicate strategically, this book is for you.

I wish all of you the best of luck in your search for the capital you need to grow your business. Put "The Home Run Hitter's Guide to Fundraising" to work and I am convinced that really working this book can increase your success in these critical meetings.

Warm Up

The New Old Game

Back in 1998 – when it was still called "The New Economy" instead of "The Bubble" – it seemed as though dot-coms couldn't open their wallets fast enough to catch all the cash flowing out of the venture capital (VC) pots of gold. The truth is that it was never that easy. Right now, at a time of renewed interest in creative business plans and start-up ideas, investors are back to assessing the viability of a young company based on business fundamentals, and not on a feeding frenzy of superheated IPO and M&A activity.

"The Home Run Hitter's Guide to Fundraising" is based on my experience helping some of the most successful business people in America to raise capital. I have coached and consulted with leaders from organizations like Ernst and Young, Mellon Capital, Microsoft, Nokia, the development team and the Dean at the Graduate School of Business at Stanford University. I have also worked with the private equity firm Hellman and Friedman JMI, as well the VC firms Mobius Capital and 3i, one of the world's largest VC firms with over 3,000 private companies in its portfolio. These companies brought me in to help their senior leaders prepare for critical communication events and develop their ability to connect, create influence, and move other people to action.

During the years of the dot-com explosion, I worked with hundreds of young companies preparing for fundraising presentations and even helped a few prepare for their IPO road shows. Partly as a result of the success of those clients,

I have been able to develop relationships with some of the very VCs and other investors you hope to get to know now. The process outlined in this book has helped entrepreneurs prepare for both one-on-one meetings with VCs on Silicon Valley's Sand Hill Road [the road with the largest contingent of VCs in Silicon Valley] and for huge VC and industry-specific forums around the country and around the world. I have helped startup and mature companies raise literally hundreds of millions of dollars of capital and close business deals worth millions more. All of this experience means that this book brings you the perspective of the people who can give your business the green light. It is battle-tested and it works.

How to use "The Home Run Hitter's Guide to Fundraising"

"The Home Run Hitter's Guide to Fundraising" synthesizes strategic planning with the power of human empathy to turn a potentially uncomfortable, unnatural presentation into an opportunity to develop and deepen an important business relationship. Because your understanding of your business and the needs of the VCs will deepen as you go, I recommend that you read through the entire process first and then go back to the start and take each section one at a time; completing the exercises that follow before proceeding to the next step. Follow this process and you will have a solid outline for a conversation that can help you close the gap between you and the people with the capital you need.

While this program will help you select the ideas you should share and teach you how to share them, ultimately the greatest strength of this book is to inform your thinking and behaving in the course of these critical meetings. The more you look at yourself as a facilitator – someone who moves a meeting towards a desired result – the greater your chances of success. This facilitation requires a kind of presence and sophistication that few inexperienced leaders have, so using the concepts in "The Home Run Hitter's Guide to Fundraising" can be a real differentiator for your leadership as well as your business.

Be ready for change. If you follow your old habits and the current industry standard, you are doomed to look and sound just like every other supplicant holding hat in hand. Stay the course. Make a connection with the *other people* in your meeting and sell what is good and right about you and your company by putting the power of "The Home Run Hitter's Guide to Fundraising" to work.

Chapter 1

Rules of the Game: The Communication Delta Model

The **Communication Delta Model** is the foundation of "The Home Run Hitter's Guide to Fundraising." It is a process for developing and delivering ideas in a way that creates predictable change in others.

Smart leaders recognize that their ability to influence depends on their ability to move other people to action. They do this through effective communication, whether by example, in conversation, via the written word or some other way. The extent to which the actions of those other people accurately reflect a leader's purpose, is a measure of successful communication and leadership.

Effective business communication creates change. The Communication Delta Model is based on the understanding that in order to get what you want, the people you talk to must change in some predictable way.

The Communication Delta Model

The delta (D) symbol in math and science represents the result, change or outcome of some process. The delta symbol is also relevant to our model because of its shape. Triangles are a strong structure both theoretically and practically. Structural engineers take advantage of that strength when they design and build bridges and skyscrapers. The Communication Delta Model is based on the premise that each side of this communication model depends on and gains strength from the others. If one side is weak, the communication will not be effective, and you will not have created predictable change in the listener. This will make it much harder, if not impossible to get the capital you're looking for.

This book is structured around the Communication Delta Model. We start first with the most important piece in the triangle, the heart of the process – the ***Result*** you must have if your meeting is going to be a success. It comes first because it drives everything that follows.

The ***Needs*** side of the triangle consists of both the needs of the VC and your needs as a businessperson and communicator. Without a clear understanding of both sets of needs, you will not connect with the people you talk to. A thorough needs assessment (in chapter 3) will help you understand the power of empathy. Without empathy, your needs will get in the way of meeting the needs of those on the other side of the table.

The ***Ideas*** side of the triangle consists of the ideas you will select to share during your meeting. Everything you say must be what that potential investor needs to hear to be willing to create the result you want. If you start planning content before you know the result you want and the needs of those you are talking to, you end up simply dumping a bunch of data on them that is probably only interesting and valuable for you.

Finally, you have to be able to deliver your ideas in a way that adds value to your company, your brand and the perception of your leadership. The ***Delivery*** side of the triangle represents the choices you must make in order to have impact, create a compelling connection, and have the influence you need in order to move that VC to change in the way you need them to.

When your ideas are result-focused, driven by the needs of the people you talk to, and delivered with impact, you have a powerful tool for change.

The Dreaded Data Dump

A Data Dump is information transmitted without a clear result. We see it every time a business executive stands up and talks for an hour about the things that only have importance to the executive. Communicating solely from the perspective of the person doing the talking will never be successful. Without a radical sensitivity to the other person, you are preaching to the converted – to and for yourself.

Having seen hundreds of pitches to potential investors, I can tell you that the Data Dump is pandemic from leaders of young companies looking for capital. Almost universally these executives stand up (or sit down) and talk about what they have invented, developed, or conceived. They talk about what their technology can do, how fast it does it, and how small they can make it. If they are lucky, the investors will listen politely while they think to themselves, "So what?" Investors are in business to make money. Smart ones, even those with deep technology backgrounds, don't care about your technology in and of itself. Sophisticated investors listen for opportunities for return on investment (ROI).

Chapter

2 Defining the Win: The Result

You're not giving a speech, you're not making a presentation. You have a very short period of time to move the people on the other side of the table to some action that gets you closer to getting capital. The Communication Delta Model helps you identify the choices you must make in order to move those potential investors to action.

The Starting Point: Defining the Result

Before you are ready to start talking or even thinking about what you are going to say to a potential investor, you have to figure out why you are talking.

Why are you having this meeting? We all understand that ultimately you want money. We also know that you won't get it in the first meeting. Until you know exactly what you want out of this particular interaction, you are not ready to put pen to paper.

First, you need to define your desired *Result*. You need to see the change in the person you are talking to as a result of the conversation you will have. From now on, as you think about any business communication, start by asking "What do I want that person to do?" instead of "What should I say?"

The first question to ask yourself is – realistically – what do you want the VC to do at the end of your meeting. Specifically, how you want them to respond, what this meeting will lead to, and how the result of this meeting will move you closer to getting your capital.

Assume you can only have one result and that result must be in the form of an action on the part of the VC. For instance:

- They will agree to meet with you again with a partner
- They will introduce you to a channel partner
- They will contact your best customer or a member of your advisory board

Any of these things can be the first step in the development of this critical relationship.

The result you select right now doesn't have to be perfect. We will come back to it when you have the additional insights you need to make sure it is realistic and appropriate.

So, the *Result* is:

What you want from a specific communication as defined by some change or action on part of the other person.

A useful device for beginning to define the *Result* for any strategic communication is to fill in the blanks in the following statement:

> When I finish this (<u>phone call, meeting, letter, voice mail, e-mail, etc.</u>), the VC will (<u>do, believe, support, call, agree, sign, meet, etc.</u>).

This *Result* statement works because it contains these key elements:

1. First, there is only one result. You build success step-by-step in a relationship. If you see someone you like at a bar, maybe having a quiet drink is enough for the first meeting. You can plan the wedding later.

2. Second, the action must be made by the VC. Seeing the result as an action by the other person forces you to look at the process with a greater sensitivity to the person who must act in order for you to succeed. The result should be something they will do, not something you will get. The difference between "my client will buy" and "I will sell" is critical. The first is

listener-focused and therefore drives content that is listener-focused. Likewise, the second is speaker-focused and ends up generating speaker-focused content.

This concept is more than just semantics or mental gymnastics. It is a critical part of making your Communication Delta structurally sound. Remember, you are working to get someone else to do something that allows you to move the business forward. Right from the start, you have to be radically focused on the other person.

3. Finally, the *Result* statement asks you to see an action or change on the part of the VC. The ideas that drive an action or change of being are very different from those driving a state of knowing or understanding. Many entrepreneurs I work with come with presentations that have an implicit result of "Understand my business plan" – and the meetings tend to fall flat. If what drives your meeting is educating the VC, you have given yourself permission to tell him everything you have time for – which leads to the data dump.

   It may be tougher than you think to limit yourself to a single, achievable result, but it is important to define this clearly. The result you want, the action you want the other person to take, must drive everything you say and everything you do or you are leaving money on the table.

Exercise: Defining the Result

Before reading further, identify a realistic result for this meeting. Remember, you are in the very early stages of this relationship. Depending on the "vetting," or the quality of the referral source or process by which an entrepreneur gets access to a VC, you need to set a conservative and obtainable result for the first meeting. Can you expect a term sheet? Not unless you are Bill Gates or Jim Clark. If you are meeting with an associate, maybe you want them to invite a partner to meet with you either now or in a future meeting. If you are meeting with a partner, perhaps you want a meeting with the partner who is most knowledgeable about the industry in which your company operates.

In following meetings, you can begin to push for greater intimacy and leverage. You might work to get that partner to start some initial due diligence by having an associate talk to your customers. If your product is functional, you can ask the VCs to test it themselves.

As you progress in the meetings with the VC, the result must become more and more involved and binding. <u>Note that for every meeting you must know exactly what you want.</u> This does not mean that you will get it or that it won't change in the course of the meeting, but it does mean that you plan, think, and strategize with that specific result in mind for that specific point in the development of the relationship.

Now, make an initial commitment to a result that will drive the content you will share in the meeting:

When I finish this meeting, the VC will ___ (Result) ______ .

You fill in the blank: Agree to another meeting? Bring in the partner who knows your space best? Spend more time with you than they had scheduled?

Don't worry about making it perfect right now; we will come back to it.

A good result is one that is based on both the needs of your business and the needs of those with the money. Get it right, even if it takes some work, and the entire process falls into place. But don't worry too much about getting it perfect; just focusing on any clear, listener-focused result will create movement and change in a positive direction.

Chapter

3 The Players: Know Your Investor, Know Yourself

Now that you've defined the result you want from this meeting, you also need a starting point. The starting point for a meeting with a VC is a clear understanding of the basis on which they will or will not make an investment. This is where empathy comes into the equation. The more time you spend walking around in their moccasins, the more insight you will have into their decision making, and the greater your chances will be of getting them to move in the direction you want them to move. Without empathy, we are back to the Data Dump.

If we are not careful, our unconscious needs will drive our actions and may drive the VC right out the door. So let's take a look at the needs of the two sets of people in this meeting. First, the needs of the VC, then yours.

Players Part I: Understanding Investors

One of the hardest things you have to understand if you are looking for VC funding for the first time, is the true nature of the relationship you are seeking. Raising venture capital is the first step in a long process of selling your business. Understanding this concept at the outset, is a powerful strategic focus.

VCs aren't looking for conventionally successful companies. They are looking for companies that will grow faster and create more value for stakeholders (including themselves) faster than the most elite early-stage businesses. Make no mistake; once you take their capital, they will own a significant piece of your business. Once a term sheet is signed, you are an executive in a corporation that reports to a board. You are no longer self-employed.

But also remember that VCs are not your enemy and they are not your competition. Companies like yours are the lifeblood of the VC world – without promising young companies to fund, VCs would not exist. However, they have to be extremely careful about the companies in which they invest. VCs are under tremendous pressure from their investors, other partners in their firm, their current portfolio, and, of course, hardworking entrepreneurs, like you, who are beating down the doors to ask for money. Failures are expensive, visible, and exhausting.

Needs Analysis for the Investor: Professional

In some ways the business of the VC is very simple. VCs are in business for one reason: to turn relatively small amounts of money into large amounts of money.

The first thing you need to understand is that VCs won't invest in most companies even if they are guaranteed to succeed. They aren't looking for companies that are simply going to do well – they are looking for companies that are going to explode in value.

Unlike banks who demand a certain percentage in return for money loaned, VCs look for **multiples**. Multiples are a way of measuring the ROI created in terms of a factor of the original investment. This means that if a VC invests one million dollars in your company in your first round of funding, they want 5, 10, or 15 X (times) that as their ROI. Why such a high multiple?

Because VCs are beholden to their investors. That's right. The folks you are turning to for money must periodically go out and ask for money themselves. VCs turn to money managers of all kinds – mutual fund managers, retirement plans, municipalities, insurance companies, and other (typically) large institutional fiduciaries and ask them to invest in a pool (e.g. fund). In other words, VCs are doing the same thing you are about to do. They say, "Let me keep some of your money for a while and I will give you a lot more back." Once a money manager invests in a Fund, he is a Limited Partner (LP).

VCs have promised their investors a return that is much, much greater than what they would get from a mutual fund or other traditional investment vehicle. They can only deliver this return if your company delivers that big multiple on the initial investment. That may sound daunting, but if you are not confident that your company will be worth five or more times an initial investment in three to five years, you are looking to the wrong source of capital.

Furthermore, even with all the due diligence, board seats taken, introductions made and capital invested, most of the companies a fund invests in will either fail outright or barely reach profitability. VCs kiss a lot of frogs before they find their prince, and therefore they have to take lots of meetings with lots of companies to find one that might be worth betting on. Most won't make it. Of the total pool of companies that a VC looks at, only about 10% get a one-on-one meeting, 2% merit the thorough evaluation process called "deep due diligence," and only about 0.5% (½ of 1%) receive funding.

That's a lot of frogs to kiss. But that is not the only frog-kissing going on. Of the 100 companies that actually get funding, traditional assumptions suggest that one company out of ten will be a home run. It's a tricky situation: VCs may hold every single company in which they invest to the high multiple criterion, but the law of the jungle suggests that most will fail, some will do OK and maybe one or two will pull the load for the entire fund. This means the that 20% ROI distributed to the fund's LPs is made up of the combined performance of all the companies in that fund's portfolio. VCs not only have to kiss a lot of frogs, they will marry a few, and most won't turn into princes no matter how much kissing they get!

The good news for you, the early-stage entrepreneur, is that the VC needs a good place to put their money almost as much as you need the money.

How does all of this information help you develop your pitch?

Nowhere does it say that a VC is commissioned to discover the next disruptive technology in wireless communication, or the smallest digital scanner, or the fastest most reliable wireless last mile solution. It is arguable that if you could show a VC how a new mouse trap manufacturing business could drive a high multiple IPO in 14 months with very little risk, you would have a good shot at getting the $40 million you need to set up plants on four continents.

VCs invest in businesses poised to dominate a big market. They do not invest in products and functionality.

Needs Analysis for the Investor: Personal

Even if you know how VC firms make money, if you are going to develop a relationship with them, you need to know who they are how they work.

VCs often have some combination of industry-specific leadership (many Sand Hill Road VCs are ex-CFOs and ex-CEOs of successful startups), investment banking with fundamental business analysis experience, and finance-oriented MBAs. The firms themselves often have a preponderance of portfolio companies from one industry or sector and the individual partners and associates usually have a core competence in one of those sectors. The job requires analytical skills as well as an ability to synthesize movements in markets and shifts/trends in technologies. They need to have the right mix of optimism and skepticism and must become good judges of character. They are competitive, smart, and do not suffer fools gladly. Good VCs sniff out real value with the sensitivity of bloodhounds. That said, they are still wrong approximately 75% of the time.

A day in the life of a VC might begin with several hours of reviewing a dozen of the executive summaries that comprise the 36-inch deep piles on their desk which they have received from "trusted sources." They may spend several more hours in back-to-back, mind-numbingly dull PowerPoint presentations by startup companies seeking capital, followed by hours of conference calls or in-house board meetings with current portfolio companies, topped off with a partners' meeting to discuss new prospective investments. If they are lucky, they may get to negotiate a term sheet (funding agreement outlining, among other things, the percentage of ownership the VC gets in exchange for the capital they give) with the attorney, CEO and CFO of a new portfolio company. While most VCs don't admit it, most don't spend time on unsolicited, "over the transom" business plans. If these unsolicited, non-vetted submissions are considered, it is usually by lower-level associates who know it is better to miss a good opportunity than it is to go to bat for a lousy one.

All VCs had better love the game of business and love the buzz of being a part of developing companies that might have a major impact on the business world. While many technology-focused VCs do love the idea of funding "The New New Thing," that love is always tempered by the reality of "The Old Old Thing" – ROI.

In short, your typical VC is:

- Smart

- Accomplished
- Professionally sophisticated
- Business savvy
- Short of time
- Has a short attention span
- Under tremendous performance pressure
- Responsible to LPs
- Risk-averse
- Looking for a needle in a haystack
- Highly accountable, visible, and responsible for his decisions
- Has other people's money on the line
- Often has deep industry/technology competence
- Must create ROI for LPs
- Must create ROI for LPs
- Must create ROI for LPs

The implications for how you will influence these people are profound.

Exercise: VC Needs

Take your own snapshot of the VCs you want to meet with by answering the following questions:

- What is the composition of their portfolio in terms of industry and sector?
- What is your vetting source; how seriously is the partner or associate taking you and this meeting?
- What is the professional background of the person with whom you will be meeting?
- How many meetings will this person have attended by the time he sees you?
- What is the multiple this firm is using as a benchmark for investment?
- What is the typical process from first meeting to term sheet?
- How soon will the firm raise another fund?

Don't know the answers to these questions? Find them. Go to their Web site. Call up executives within their portfolios and ask them. Call partners within the firm, or other firms with whom they often syndicate deals (make joint investments). The more time and effort you spend looking at the world from the investor's viewpoint, the more power you will have to <u>select the ideas that are most likely to have impact on them</u>.

Players Part II: Know Yourself

Now that you have a clear picture of the key drivers for the VC, you are almost ready to start thinking about what you will say to them. But first you have to do some of the hardest research of all: you have to look honestly and objectively at yourself and your business.

Why do so many business meetings feel like Data Dumps? Because most of us communicate wearing mirrored blinders. Not only are we limited in our range of vision, but most of what we see is a reflection of our own needs. Data Dumps happen when an entrepreneur organizes everything he knows about his business and talks about it regardless of the value or interest to the VC.

Presentations about a business, developed to help others understand what you do and how you do it, are doomed to be Data Dumps. Especially when you let PowerPoint drive the planning, you have the current – lousy – industry standard. They all look alike. They all feel alike and they do absolutely nothing to help you sell your business.

If you want to have real influence over others, you have to communicate with a radical sensitivity to the people you are talking to. A radical sensitivity to the other person means that the listener's needs drive everything you do and everything you say.

But the other person's needs as opposed to what?

In this instance, it is The VCs' needs as opposed to your needs - the needs of the entrepreneur leading the meeting.

If you do not realize how your own subconscious drivers influence your decisions, you risk letting your needs drive your communication. Remember, in your meeting, it won't matter what you want or need. What matters is what drives the choices the VC makes.

Some of your needs are conscious and clearly understood by all parties – your desire to grow the business and your need for capital. Some are physiological, like the ones I will discuss at the end of this book on managing the fight or flight response. Some are unconscious, neurotic and even self-destructive. But whatever they are, and wherever they come from, if you are not aware of them, you can't manage them. The better you know yourself – in any context – the better able you are to connect with, meet the needs of, and ultimately influence other people. This is critically important as you plan what to say and how to say it in your meetings with VCs.

Let's do a needs analysis for you, the entrepreneur. What follows are a range of unspoken needs that, left unmanaged, can get in the way of you meeting the needs of the people you talk to.

Your Needs: Professional

Capital Hungry: You need to raise capital for your business. The challenge is to make sure that your appetite for capital doesn't rob you of your ability to meet the needs of the VC. The entrepreneur/VC relationship is not an adversarial one, but when you want something that someone else has (capital), the tendency is to project an adversarial element into it. When competitive people get into adversarial relationships they try to win. If your attitude reflects your need to win this meeting instead of your desire to convince your VC of the value of your company as an investment, you run the risk of appearing defensive, and maybe even hostile.

Pride: You and your engineers have worked your rear ends off developing a tool that actually does something powerful. You have every right to be proud of what you have developed. You also need to understand that the functional power of your technology or product has very little to do with the quality of the business as a potential investment. Products and solutions have relatively short lives. Great businesses can live, prosper, and create value for a long time. I can't tell you the number of times I have personally heard VCs say, "We don't invest in technology, we invest in businesses."

Your Needs: Personal

Professional needs are often conscious and therefore easier to manage than other types of needs. Personal needs are often harder to assess because they are sometimes completely subconscious. But if you want to have real impact on other people, you have to find a way to see yourself the way they see you.

Intellectual: I have coached and consulted with many leaders of VC-backed companies who are great problem solvers and quick thinkers. Along with competence and a measure of success, however, often comes an ego. Having a strong sense of who you are and what you are capable of is a great asset. However, if your need to convince a VC how smart you are overshadows your ability to give that investor what they need, you may be the smartest person in America who never gets funded.

Highly intelligent people often use vocabulary that only has meaning for an extremely small segment of the world's population. If you are describing your market, your product or the nature of your solution in language only relevant to industry insiders, you risk creating an understanding gap between you and the VC. The latest industry and company buzzwords and acronyms fall into this category.

I am convinced that if you can't explain something to my grandmother who is turning 100 next year and still uses a rotary phone, then A: you aren't ready to pitch it because B: you don't really understand your value proposition that well.

Snobbery, whether intellectual or social, is never attractive. The person who can explain a complex idea in simple terms appears to understand it better than someone who leans on the latest jargon.

Delta Law of Communication Responsibility:
The person doing the talking is responsible for helping the person doing the listening to understand, follow and take action. It is never the listener's job to make the talker's job easier.

Financial: The fact that you need money for a new roof or a new car may be driving your ambition, but if it drives your content or (as we will see later) your delivery, you can appear like you are pleading. You look like you're powerless and project yourself into a position of lower status in the professional hierarchy. If everything you say and everything you do doesn't look and sound as if you have a right to be there, you will be leaving money on the table.

Physical Security: If you let your discomfort drive your content and delivery, you will most likely seem needy, weak, and unsure. VCs, like the rest of us, make an instantaneous assessment of you as you walk into their office. Part of obeying the Delta Law of Communication Responsibility suggests that you must make the choices that help you look and sound like the leader you are (or can be).

Many conscious and subconscious needs can influence your ability to develop and deepen a relationship with a potential investor. Consider the following as you work to bracket your needs out of the planning process in order to select the ideas that are radically results-oriented and focused on the needs of your VC.

***Needs* to Explore:**

- Need to win
- External competitive pressure creating urgency
- Comfort
- Control
- Power
- Need to please
- Wanting to be perceived as friendly
- Not wanting to seem pushy
- Not wanting to seem weak
- Fear of showing ignorance
- Need to be right

- Need to perform
- Need to meet the needs of teammates
- Need to make a million dollars before you are thirty
- Need to be the youngest, oldest, first woman, man, etc. to do X
- Need to earn more than your classmates, your father, etc.
- Need to seem older or younger

Our needs are neither good nor bad. They just are. In some combination, they make us who we are. Absent some mechanism for assessing our own sometimes hidden needs, however, they can become powerful obstacles for achieving both professional and personal goals. As the old Zen maxim goes, "the only real mastery is self mastery." Look at yourself as objectively as you can. Ask those closest to you for feedback on specific issues and let them know that honesty is the only way for you to get the results you are after. Hire a therapist or a coach if you need to. Know yourself better and you will be better able to get results as a business communicator and as a leader.

Needs Exercise: Entrepreneur

Take 10 minutes to make a list of the issues that might be driving your choices as a communicator. Don't edit. Just write down what is important to you right now for both your business and personal life. Once you have written them down, keep them with you as you begin to outline the ideas you chose to share with an investor. This will help you judge whether you are focused on the VC or on yourself as a communicator.

Chapter

4 Game Plan: Part 1. What you Say

Okay. You have defined the result you want in terms of some change or action on the part of the person you are meeting with. You have also built the first side of the triangle because you know what drives the VC and you have taken the time to look objectively at yourself in order to make sure his needs are driving the process, not yours. But it's not enough to just know your audience or know yourself. You have to use those insights to make sure that everything you say and everything you do is based on what the VCs need to experience in order for them to go where you want them to go. This is how empathy becomes a strategic tool and helps you make a critical connection. Connecting and creating change is what business communication is all about.

You have to start building the second side of the triangle. You do this by thinking about your result together with the VCs needs and select the ideas they need to hear so that they are willing do what you want them to do. These ideas – words, images, analogies, and stories – are the second side of the Communication Delta Model.

Your Core Message: The Hook

A good way to start thinking about ideas is to ask yourself: "What must this VC believe if they are going to do what I want them to do?" Based on the needs you know a VC has, what can you promise to deliver that has real value for an investor?

Your core message is a *Hook* that says to the VC:

<u>Do what I want you to do and I will give you what I know you need.</u>

You must know exactly what that particular VC needs and you must have a solution that specifically meets that need. Otherwise you are swinging blind.

Your *Hook* should come near the beginning of your talk; it might even function as your opening. Before you get very far into your meeting, you need to articulate your core value proposition and why they should listen to you carefully. A successful *Hook* moves your potential investor to action by delivering the necessary information:

- **WIFM**, or "**W**hat's **I**n **I**t **F**or **M**e": Tells the VC what's in it for them to do your *Result* and gives them a reason to listen by identifying your...
- **Core Value Proposition**: which tells the VC how your solution will create ROI for their LPs while making...
- **A powerful request** that tells them what they have to do to get their *WIFM* and...
- **Raises questions** in their minds, the answers to which become your supporting content.

Let's look at these one at a time.

WIFM: Your *Hook* must tell a potential investor why they should do what you want them to do, based on what you know is most important to them. With the venture community, if the *WIFM* does not clearly relate to ROI, you'd better have a really good reason why not (for instance, they only fund nonprofits focused on ecological restoration).

Core Value Proposition: Your core value proposition describes the problem your product or service solves with a radical sensitivity to the needs of an investor. It is not enough to say, "We make wireless routers." If your *Hook* is going to work, it has to suggest the opportunity for the investor: "Our unique wireless routing solution saves our customers $1,000 a month over our competitor's solution."

Powerful Request: If this investor wants access to the opportunity your solution provides, they have to do what you want them to do. If, for instance, your *Result* is for them to perform some initial due diligence, you might say: "The more you know about our company, the more compelling this investment opportunity becomes." It may not be subtle, but it tells them you know what they need and what they need to do to get it.

Raises Questions: During your meeting, you will have to say more than just your *Hook*. When you have 30 minutes instead of 30 seconds, you not only have to suggest that your company is a good investment, you need to prove it. The content that supports your *WIFM* and your *Powerful Request* falls explicitly from the words you use in your *Hook*. Your supporting content, the bulk of the ideas you select to share during your meeting with a VC, are literally the answers to the questions that a good *Hook* creates for the people you are talking to.

The Hook – Explicit or Implicit

Depending on how the first few minutes of the meeting flow, it may not be necessary nor helpful to recite the words exactly as they are written out. That being said, You should find a way to work the actual words of the *Hook* into the conversation near the beginning because those ideas must be planted firmly in the mind of the investor. It is better to seem a bit rehearsed than not get the core ideas of the *Hook* out there. If the VC hears and understands your *core value proposition*, your *powerful promise*, the *WIFM* for the investor to do your *Result* and the *right questions* in the organic course of conversation, then go with it. But if you are not sure you have really set your *Hook*, take the opportunity to say:

> *I want to make sure that you understand that this company will lap the field in the $40B wireless router space and we want to take you with us. We will be a highly profitable $100M business in 24 months. But you will have to know more about us than this half-hour meeting will allow.*

Find ten different ways to get your message out there conversationally. The more fluent you are with the intersection between your *Result* and the investor's *WIFM*, the more confident you will be when questions start coming from left field. Try not to think of this as a presentation. It would be great if you never made another presentation. Even with 1,000 people in your audience, the more that what you say seems like an important conversation, the more impact you will have.

The ultimate test of your *Hook* is this: If the VC believes the promise of the *WIFM*, they will give you your desired result. If you are convinced they will, then all you have to do with content is convince them you can deliver on that promise. You do that by answering the questions your *Hook* generates.

Excavating Content: Answering the Hook's Questions

So how much is too much to say and how do you know what to share? You have lots to say about your company and so little time. How do you organize your thoughts in a way that helps you achieve your result?

You don't organize, you select. Organizing is a prescription for the Data Dump. Your *Hook* has already done the heavy lifting in the process of distilling the ideas you must share in order to convince an investor that you can deliver. If you find yourself inventing questions that you want to answer – "they might want to know about this, I can't leave this out" – then you are probably back to being driven by your own need to tell versus the VCs need to hear.

Remember that the final benefit of a good *Hook* is that it raises questions in the minds of the people who hear it. Why is that such a big deal?

You don't want to leave a potential investor full of questions, right? Actually, some unanswered questions are critical to the development of the relationship. Remember that saying everything you know is a Data Dump. But the questions arising directly from your *Hook* actually define what you say in the rest of this meeting.

Let's return to the router company *Hook* as an example.

> *When you really kick the tires on our team and our technology, I am convinced you will find that this company will lap the competition in the $40B wireless router space. We will be a $100M company with 40% margins in 24 months.*

The *Result* for the investor is to "really kick the tires," or initiate some due diligence that is the next step toward making an investment.

The *WIFM* for the VC is the ROI on an early-stage company growing from virtually nothing to one valued based on the market and an estimate of how big you project the business will be. This is one reason you want to give them some idea of the scale early on – it gives them a reason to listen. If the projections are reasonable, based on their understanding of the industry and sector, and large enough to get them seeing dollar signs, then they are more likely to give you their undivided attention.

First, identify where you want them to go:

> **When you really kick the tires**... Identifies the result – where you want the VC to go – and raises the question:

- What do I have to do to "Kick the tires"? Answer: Start some initial due diligence.

Then tell them why your company will succeed based on their definition of success.

...**on our team and technology**...raises the questions:

- What's so great about your team?
- What is your technology?

...**this company will lap the competition**...

- What are your competitive advantages and barriers to entry in your product class?

...**in the $40B wireless router space...**

- Where did the $40b market come from?

...**we will be a $100MM company with 40% margins in 24 months**...

- How will you drive $100mm in revenue with 40% margins in 24 months?

You now have five or six key questions that have to be answered if you are going to move the VC to action. What most people call the content of a presentation is really nothing more than the answers to the questions that flow directly from your *Hook*. Developing content this way is critical for making these meetings strategic and *results-focused*. Your *Hook* tells the VC what he has to do for the opportunity to look more closely at a company that might create the returns they are looking for. If you stick to answering the questions that directly fall out of the *Hook*, then your content will further convince the VC that you can deliver on the promise the *Hook* implicitly makes – that the VC will make money by investing in your company.

This stage of the planning process requires extra vigilance and discipline. At this point in the process, entrepreneurs often feel a powerful pull into the black hole of the Data Dump. Even with faith in the process, the desire to talk about how long it has taken you to write the code, the cool functionality of your product, the thousands of applications the product has, how progressive the culture of your company is, etc. can be overpowering. But all of that content is driven by the needs of the wrong person in this conversation. Anything that is not radically listener-focused risks confusing the VC or convincing them that you don't have your eye on the prize. Remember, the prize for professional investors is making lots of money.

A good *Hook* serves several critical strategic roles in developing communication that moves listeners to action.

> **First**: A good *Hook* gives the listener a reason to pay attention. It clearly identifies *WIFM* from the receiver's point of view.
>
> **Second**: A good *Hook* identifies, implicitly or explicitly what the listener has to do (the *result*) in order to get *WIFM*.
>
> **Third**: A good *Hook* leaves certain questions unanswered in the listener's mind. The answers to those unanswered questions, and only those answers, becomes the content of the communication.

Hook: This new marketing program is the key to making this quarter's earnings goal.

- *Deliverer's Result*: The listener will accept the new marketing program.
- *WIFM*: Making the quarterly earnings goal.
- *Unanswered Questions*:
  - What is the new marketing program?
  - Why is it the key to making the quarterly earnings goal?
  - How will it help us make the goal?

A good *Hook* motivates the listener to act on the *desired Result*. If he hears the *Hook* and says, "So what?" then you have the wrong *WIFM* and need to do more research.

If the listener buys in and is excited but doesn't act on the result, then your *Hook* did not clearly align with the *WIFM* for that listener.

Hook Exercise:

Look at the following *Hooks* and identify:

- The deliverer's desired *Result*
- The listener's *WIFM*
- The questions that must be answered to move the listeners to the *Result*

"This strategy is the key to increasing market share."

Result: Listeners will ____________________.

WIFM (for listener) ______________________

?____

? _______________________________________

? _______________________________________

"Accepting this order now means more profits tomorrow."

Result: Listeners will ___________________.

WIFM (for listener) ______________________

?_______________________________________

? ______________________________________

? ______________________________________

"Let me come back on Thursday and I'll show you how we can improve your ratings."

Result: Listeners will ___________________.

WIFM (for listener) ______________________

?_______________________________________

? ______________________________________

? ______________________________________

"A real coaching relationship is the key to lower turnover."

Result: Listeners will ___________________.

WIFM (for listener) ______________________

?_______________________________________

? ______________________________________

? ______________________________________

Content and Your Hook: Looping back to the Heart

Your *Hook* is the heart of your content. As you evaluate the quality of the ideas you choose to share, ask yourself, "Must the people in this meeting hear this now in order to believe my *Hook*?" If the answer is no, then that idea is probably information near and dear only to you and therefore part of a Data Dump. Use the following questions as a reality check:

- Does the way you are talking about your product create a perception of value from an investment standpoint, or are you bragging about your beloved pet project?
- Do the members of your team sound like business school graduates or leaders of a company that will dominate a huge market?
- Do your financial projections support the scale an investor will need, or are you showing us that your accountant is a star at Excel?

If you can't close the loop from your ideas to the *WIFM* for your listeners, that content will probably take you further and further away from the result you want.

Supporting Content Exercise:

Answering the Questions

Write down your Hook. Using the words and key ideas it encapsulates, identify the questions that flow from it.

***Tip**: If your Hook is half a page long and 20 questions fall from it, you are dumping data. Remember, you are only working to achieve one thing – whatever you have identified as* *your Result. The Hook should be just what the VC needs to hear for them to want to do that specific thing.*

At this point, an outline should begin to take shape. Hopefully it looks something like this:

Hook: When you really kick the tires on our team and our technology, I am convinced you will find that this company will lap the competition in the $40B wireless router space. We will be a $100M company with 40% margins in 24 months.

Questions from the *Hook*:

- Who is on your team?
  Answer
  Answer
  Answer

- What is your technology?
  Answer
  Answer
  Answer

- What are your competitive advantages and barriers to entry in your product class?
  Answer
  Answer
  Answer

- Where did the $40b market come from?
  Answer
  Answer
  Answer

- How will you drive $100m in revenues with 40% margins (describe your revenue and profit models) in 24 months?

Answer
Answer
Answer

Make sure you are developing these ideas with the same sensitivity to the VCs interests and needs that you used for your *Hook*. The fact that your team has a combined experience of 100 years is nowhere near as important as the fact that each brings leadership experience where he or she developed a leading solution in a similar space and led it, for instance, to a high-multiple IPO.

As you start filling in your blanks, continue to ask yourself, "What makes these ideas valuable to a potential investor?" Let your content answer the questions that flow from your *Hook*, focus the answers on the needs of your potential investor, and your content is now as strategic as the rest of the process.

The Prep: An Opening That Sows the Seeds

Entrepreneurs are often surprised that they don't start the planning process with a snappy opening. The truth is you should not plan your opening until you have your *Hook* and your supporting ideas developed. You want to make sure that everything you say, including your opening or what is called your *Prep*, is a part of the strategic process of convincing VCs that you can deliver on the promise you make in your *Hook*. As the term implies, your *Prep* is there to prepare the VC to hear your message, but you want your *Hook* and your supporting ideas to drive your *Prep*, not the other way around.

Remember, this is not a presentation. You are having a business meeting with intelligent, busy people who are under lots of pressure. It is very unlikely that you will want to use a dramatic story or confetti-filled balloons, and please, don't start with a video clip or Web-based demonstration. At least not until they ask you for it.

The most effective way to open these meetings is to create a context for the solution by simply describing the size, the immediacy and the cost associated with the problem you are planning to solve. The bigger the problem and the pain associated with it, the better.

Prep Example: Describe the Problem

Right now, millions of network users are tied to their desks and their desktops if they want the immediacy of information exchange and the security the networks provide for them. Your partners have to carry password generators that silently become obsolete or you have to remember dozens of keystrokes to get on protected networks. When you can't get to the office, even if you have computers on the road or in the home, most likely you have to throw away full days of productivity. It costs the financial services industry alone over 4 billion dollars a year. The total problem in the US is at least 10 times that number and larger still around the world. Until our solution, it was considered an unsolvable issue. We have solved this problem in an elegant and compelling way and... [here comes the hook]...

when you really kick the tires on our team and our technology, I am convinced you will find that this company will lap the competition in the $40B wireless router space. We will be $100M company with 40% margins in 24 months.

In this example, there is an opening to which the VC can personally relate. The more real you can make the issue or problem your company solves, the more engaged they will become in this journey.

The function of the *Prep* segment is to prepare the listener for your *Hook*. It is not an excuse to tell a joke or a funny story. It is not necessarily time to loosen up the audience or the speaker. If a joke or funny story helps get the receiver ready – great, if it helps the speaker loosen up, that is a secondary side benefit. If, however, everyone is loose and happy and no one hears the *Hook*, then your personal wishes are driving your choices, not the *Result* or the needs of the investor.

Different situations require different *Preps*. A presentation to thousands of employees at an annual company meeting may require an explosion of energy. A phone call asking for a meeting clearly needs a different type of introduction.

What follows are suggestions and guidelines for the *Prep*. Each situation must be evaluated individually, always in the context of the *Result*, the *Needs* and the *Hook*.

- **Prep With Your *Hook***
  Some communications require you to hit hard and hit fast. To veteran sales staff, for instance, you might simply say:

  The key to making your sales goal is focusing on new customers.

  Note: This may be a good way to start with the VC

community. This type of *Prep* tends to be pretty strong and you must be able to express real confidence to pull this off.

- **Establish Common Ground**
  You need this audience to believe that you have been in their shoes and understand their needs before they will hear your *Hook*. To an exhausted assembly line crew just before another round of quality improvement:

  Before I got into management, I spent 15 years working my way up on the shop floor. Every year it seemed like some new productivity program would make my job harder and more complex.

- **Bring Them Up To Speed**
  Some of your listeners do not understand what has happened in this situation up to now. You can bring them up in an opening.

  As many of you know, we are now in the fourth year of a five-year implementation. Up to now, we have been delighted with the results of this process, but we have one hurdle left to overcome.

  Note: Be careful not to patronize or overly summarize. If you know everyone is up to speed, choose another *Prep* type.

- **Shock Them Awake**
  Sometimes your receivers need to be challenged and shaken up a bit to be ready to hear the *Hook*. Speaking to the American Psychological Society, you might get them ready for the *hook* by saying:

  We all know that the talking cure is a waste of time. One third of your patients get better, one third get worse, and one third stay the same.

  Note: Your *Hook* had better let them know you are on their side.

- **Come Clean**
  Some times the only way to establish true rapport and get people ready to hear your *Hook* is to be brutally honest and say what no one thinks you can say. Here I am trying to convince a security analysts group to give the company's stock another chance.

  I wish I could say we met our earnings goal this quarter, but we did not.

- **The Standards**
  Define a word: *Webster's defines efficiency as ...*

  Give an anecdote or story: *On the way to this meeting I met a homeless person asking for money...*

  Tell A Joke: *Three religious leaders were in a boat: a rabbi, a Catholic priest and a Baptist preacher...*

  Note: I call them standards because we hear them time and time again. If it's not fresh, funny, and inoffensive to everyone in the meeting and focused on your *Hook*, don't use it.

Be aware that no matter how you choose to start a communication, if you don't *Prep* them for your *Hook*, you may confuse your audience and risk them missing the *Hook* altogether. When that happens, it will be harder to get the *Result* you want.

Prep Don'ts:

- Don't fumble with your laptop and projector for five minutes while the VC goes for their fourth cup of coffee.
- Don't distribute a 20-page color document of your presentation and ask them not to skip ahead.

- Don't open PowerPoint if you can help it (although some VC are so used to bad presentations that they now demand them)
- Don't start with a ten minute historical overview of your company, your mission statement, your current capitalization tables, or the 49ers' chances of getting to the Super Bowl. The quicker you give them a reason to believe you can create a high multiple return, the quicker you will get funded.

I hope you realize that you won't say your *Prep* at the end of the meeting – you will say it at the beginning. But in order to create a strategic *Prep*, – just like the rest of your content – it is developed from your *Hook*. In fact, sometimes you can simply open with your *Hook*. It depends on who you are talking to, how much time you have, and what you know about what that investor is looking for.

The Close

You know the *Result* you want for this particular meeting. You have researched the VC and you know what they are looking for. You have greater insight into your hidden needs that might get in the way of connecting with that investor. You have a *Hook* that brings all of that together in a powerful statement that makes a promise and a powerful request and drives the supporting content. You open with your *Prep*, drive the *Hook* and convince them with your supporting ideas. Then you thank them for their time and go off to your next appointment, right?

Only if you want to make it really easy for that VC to forget all about you.

These investors sometimes sit through a dozen or more early-stage company pitches a day. Even if they were jumping out of their seats when they were with you, chances are they won't remember you or your solution by the end of the day. Your job is to get these people to take some action, remember? So at the end of the meeting, you must ask them to do what you want them to do.

This process is about selling a big chunk of your company. If you have ever had any sales training, you know about the importance of closing. If you haven't, let me be the first to tell you: You have to close!

In the old methodology, the "closing section" was the place for a summary. Summaries remind people of the most interesting or important points you went over with the assumption that getting the other person to remember your ideas was the goal. As you know by now, this is not the real goal.

You don't care whether they remember anything you said. You only care about whether they are willing to do your *Result*!

Arguably, thousands of potential deals have been left on the table because no one asked for the order.

The *Close* serves a strategic function in communication by asking the listener to do your *Result*. It can happen in one of two ways.

- **Ask for the Order:** Directly ask your listeners to do your Result.

  Ladies and gentlemen, when you leave here today you have a choice to make. I ask that you vote in favor of the measure I have described.

- ***Hook* 'em Again:** Remind them of the *WIFM* by restating your *Hook*. If your *Result* is explicit enough in your *Hook,* the VC should either say, "Great, let's get you on the calendar" or "I don't see it. Best of luck."

  For all of these powerful reasons, I think you will agree that the key to making your quarterly goal is implementing this new program.

You must decide which is best depending on the *Result* and the *Needs* of the investor.

A Note on Summarizing

Remember that part of the power of this process is the ability to move the receiver to action. If, at the end of this communication, you revert to an old-fashioned summary, you lose a golden opportunity to remind them of their *WIFM* and to ask for the *Result*. A summary is a Data Dump with no action at the end. You may, however, briefly summarize the most powerful reasons for doing the *Result* before you *Close*.

You should close directly. First, restate the *Hook, then* ask directly what more they need before they move forward.

Close as concretely as you can. Get them to agree to a date, or have them get you to the person who does their scheduling. Move things as far as you can and as explicitly as you can.

This does two important things: it keeps you and your company from falling through the administrative cracks, and it shows that you are a businessperson who knows how to close a deal. Both bode well for the future of your business.

Always *Close* for something. If it is clear they aren't interested, ask them for 10-minute debrief on what more or different they needed. Ask them if they would recommend or – better still – refer you to the resource that would make you more attractive as an investment or to an investor who might be more interested. One way or the other, move it forward. Even if you are disappointed (and you probably will be, many times before you get your capital) look for the opportunity to get some value from the time and the relationship.

Exercise: The Close

Decide whether you will close them directly or indirectly, then write down your closing statement and know it by heart. While I typically don't advocate memorizing, this is one piece of content you need to be very comfortable saying. You never know when you will get a closing opportunity.

NOTE You have to be ready to move the relationship forward based on what the VC is giving you – regardless of where you are in the process.

Key Content Areas: Attributes of a Great Business, Not a Great Presentation

I have had the good fortune to work with experienced VCs, corporate attorneys and successful entrepreneurs on coaching teams preparing entrepreneurs for important VC meetings and public forums. The general consensus from these insiders is that investors need to know a handful of core issues about your business if you want to be taken seriously.

- **Problem**: What is the pain your product or service reduces? The more dire, obvious, expensive, and ubiquitous the pain or problem is, the better.

- **Solution**: Specifically, how does your product or service reduce that pain or solve that problem? It is not enough to say that you can. You must be able to explain how – simply, concisely and with confidence.

- **Market Size**: The basic question is this: In a competitive environment, does the market exist to drive a high-multiple return assuming you can get a realistic percentage of that market? VCs know the difference between a market defined by the entire universe of opportunity in an industry – software – and the actual market your solution can reasonably capture – accounting software for small businesses. You won't dazzle a potential investor with a trillion-dollar market opportunity if you can only realistically hope to capture half a million. If the scale isn't there, the multiple isn't there, and the professional VCs won't be interested. This does not mean that your business can't make you rich – it just means that the VC world is probably not the right place to look for capital.

- **Economic Engine/Revenue Model/Special Sauce**: What is special about your go-to-market strategy? What is uniquely valuable to the investment potential of your business about the way you will penetrate your market? What is your "special sauce," that is, why will you grow faster, bigger and at lower cost than your competition or the currently available solution?

- **Team**: It is apocryphal that the due diligence mantra for the venture community changed between 1999 and 2001 from "Team, Technology, Market" to "Team, Team, Team." Apocryphal because truly great leadership teams always figure out a way to make money even in tough markets and investors have always known this is true. If you and your buddies from undergraduate school have stumbled onto the solution to a huge, expensive business problem, you are well-advised to find a few "grey hairs" who would be willing to lend their expertise and their endorsement to the enterprise. It is a hard but fair reality that many investors use the experience and historical success of a young company's leadership as the single most important prognosticator of future success. If you don't have solid leadership already on board, some VCs will help you find it, but it will absolutely be at the expense of your equity and control. Without a track record of success, your demands to remain at the helm no matter what, will often be ample justification for a potential investor to say "Next!" Teams matter because investors know that the only mantra that really works in business is "execute, execute, execute," and that is all about people.

- **Competitive Advantage and Barriers to Entry**: Investors want to know how you compare to the other choices your customers have and how you are going to make it harder for copycats to take your ideas and run with them. First to market, patents, deep existing relationships with critical customers and channel partners are all useful in making a case for the security of your competitive turf. That said, the only real barriers to entry and competitive advantage are the creativity, passion and energy of the people running a business. The investor must make a gut judgment about whether you can keep a business out front or not.

This is by no means a comprehensive list of what you must address in every VC meeting, but some version of this list keeps coming up in conversation with industry insiders – and for good reason. Great businesses are consistently defined by the right combination of these issues and attributes. Since most startups don't have profits, free cash flows or even revenues, the metrics used for the analysis of mature companies are replaced by the analysis of some combination of the items on this list.

Look at this list before a potential investor does and do your own rough analysis of the strength and potential strength of your company in relationship to it. Early-stage investors don't expect you to have all the answers, nor do they need a company to be perfect before it raises capital. But understanding what investors are looking for helps you both to focus your remarks on the strengths you have and to get out there and build the strength you need.

The Elevator Pitch: 30 Seconds to Fame and Glory

As an entrepreneur, you are constantly being thrust into mythical elevators alone with a potential investor who is going up 20 floors in two minutes. The fantasy is that if you don't give the VC a reason to want to learn more by the time they reach their stop, you will have blown your one golden opportunity. A tough ride for both of you.

Back in the bubble days, you could enter elevator pitch competitions (some still exist today). Each contest organizer had its own arcane rules and ideas on what must be articulated to stand a chance to win a round of golf at Silverado with the VC of your dreams. Organizers saw nothing wrong with entrepreneurs developing a 20-slide PowerPoint presentation for a two-minute micro pitch. Never mind that it took longer than the mythical elevator ride to boot up the average laptop. It was fantasy gone mad.

The value of an elevator pitch is not to test how much information you can cram into two minutes. Elevator pitches are terrific indicators of how well you understand your business from the perspective of potential investors, customers, partners, etc. If you can't engage someone – whomever they may be to your business – in a sentence or two, then you don't understand your business well enough to be able to deliver a *WIFM*.

A good elevator pitch is a distillation of your *Result*, the *WIFM* and the most compelling answers to the questions that fall from your *Hook*. This forces you to think strategically and surgically excise the fat from the core of your value proposition. You have to bring the strength of your company together with the needs of your listeners and you have to do it fast. Developing a handful of these pithy little marvels is a great exercise in deepening your own understanding of what you are in business for and for helping you to connect with a wide range of critical outside partners.

As with many business pop culture phenomena, the elevator pitch madness has a basis in a real value-added process. Samuel Clemens - AKA Mark Twain - once apologized for the length of a correspondence with, "I would have written a shorter letter but I didn't have time." Saying something meaning- fully in a few words is much more difficult than prattling on for hours.

Here are a few paraphrased examples drawn from my work with one client as we worked to pare his company's story to a bare minimum of words for different situations.

> *Security and poor power management cost American business $X billion a year and residences another $Y billion. COMPANY-NAME gives residences and business complete remote control over*

the security and efficiency of buildings and operations. With a team like the '93 Chicago Bulls representing a track record of repeated start-up-to-liquidity success for investors, COMPANY-NAME is poised to make early partners runaway champions in the ROI game. Let me tell you more about this exciting technology and investment opportunity.

I can say this slowly in 35 seconds. It works because it asks for the suspension of disbelief on critical issues for investors: scale, problem/solution, leadership and ROI.

Need it said in 20 seconds?

By giving X billion corporate and residential customers Remote Control over the $X billion headaches that are security and utility management from just about any wireless communication device, COMPANY-NAME's proven leadership team brings a high-multiple opportunity to early investors and partners. Come learn more.

Still get the *WIFM* and the *Result*, just a shorter elevator ride.

So what does my client say at a cocktail party when someone asks him what he does for a living? Say he is the CEO of a startup that helps companies manage security and utility costs? No. He says, "*I am the CEO of Company X. We allow our customers to use cell phones and Blackberries to save their corporations and residences millions in security and utility losses."*

The focus is not on what the company makes, but what it does for customers and investors.

Elevator Pitch Exercise:

As leaders of a new company, the elevator pitch is worth the time and effort. Good elevator pitches often become the blueprint for statements of mission, tag lines and branding elements. Until you can say it succinctly for half a dozen audiences, you don't really understand what you are selling.

Identify four critical audiences (VCs, customers, channel partners, prospective directors) and develop a 30-second distillation of the value your business represents to each of their individual needs. It should take two or three iterations before you really boil it down to pure value. Then practice saying it out loud, slowly, and record it. Listen to yourself and see if it sounds conversational and real. If not, write another iteration using language that is authentic for you. When the words you recorded are compelling for each listener and sound like you talking, you are ready to answer the question: "What does your business do?"

Chapter

5 Game Plan: Part 2: What You Show

I had a client who had a series of meetings with a world-class VC in New York whom she had been warned would expect to sit back and listen to a standard PowerPoint presentation. Essentially he was saying, "I want you to make it easy for me to say no to you." After experiencing some pretty dramatic results using the approach I am laying out here, she was damned if she was going to fly all the way to New York in order to have a boring, uninspired meeting with this guy.

So she took her laptop with her, onto which was loaded a handful of useful slides, but before she opened it she said, "Before I get started with my pitch, I want to give you a 30,000-feet overview of what we are doing." Then she stood up and made a simple diagram of the problem her company solved and how they solved it. Two hours later in a meeting scheduled for half an hour, she still had not opened her laptop and the guy she was meeting with had hardly sat down because he got so involved in adding to and poking holes in her plan.

She got her capital!

Business people vastly overuse presentation graphics and nowhere is this truer than in the VC pitch. VCs themselves sometimes ask for information on your company in the form of a PowerPoint file. The problem is this is about the same thing as an HR director asking for you to send a resume – it makes it easy to say no. VCs simply wait until they get the document or the file, look for some small element that justifies taking you out of the running (typo, market size, anything they choose), have an administrative assistant call and drop the ax.

Because they are almost never the result of a strategic planning process, graphics-heavy presentations always get between you and the VC. You are not being told to leave out visuals in your meeting, but there are good and bad reasons to use visuals and good and bad ways of using them.

Lousy Reasons to Use Graphics

Most entrepreneurs use visual support for the wrong reason. But whether it is fear, haste or following the Joneses, make sure you don't fall into any of these traps as you complete the *Ideas* side of the communication triangle.

Lousy Reason 1: You need something to hide behind.

Executives in just about every business situation these days rely too heavily on graphics. It may be that folks get a greater sense of security if they don't have to see the faces in the audience and they may feel more comfortable with their content projected onto a screen for them and everyone else to see. This process robs you of your ability to have real impact and connect with a VC.

You worked hard to get the meeting with the VC in order to develop and deepen a relationship with someone you hope will become one of the most important members of your team. You wouldn't give a PowerPoint presentation on your life and family on a first date. You might show pictures of your friends and family at some point, but first you have to get a sense of chemistry. An early meeting with an investor is similar. Don't use PowerPoint to avoid what you came for – a connection.

Lousy Reason 2: Everyone else does it this way.

Actually, they don't. The most confident, experienced business communicators don't rely on pre-set presentation graphics because they know the best of these meetings may take unpredictable turns. Many of my clients purposefully jump up and diagram ideas that need to be made visually on a white board or a flip chart. The reason this process works better in many situations is that the visuals that come out of it are immediate, spontaneous, and are typically in response to a need that listeners may have about the ideas you are sharing.

If you think about the most important conversations or meetings in your life, I would bet that not many of them included a digital projection unit. In fact, even in business the most sophisticated, confident and effective communicators don't use graphic-driven presentations. But here is the real kicker. In a world of PowerPoint-wielding frogs, the brave soul working to make a connection based on a mutual proposition of real value will look and sound like a handsome prince. One of your big hurdles with the VC community is to be remembered, and using a software program that comes preloaded on just about every Windows PC on the planet does nothing to differentiate you.

Many presenters at industry and venture forums actually prescribe the use of PowerPoint (down to the number of slides) – not because the graphics add value, but because they give the forum facilitators a modicum of control over the density and arguably the quality of the presentation. Read between the lines and you will see that the instructions from the forums do not require you to use graphics and that time allotments are maximums not minimums. Every now and then you will see some brave CEO (often of the serial success variety) stand up with no visual support and he will get pin-drop silence during the talk, a standing ovation and top marks for the presentation. That is what leadership looks like and it is worth working and preparing for.

Lousy Reason 3: You need help remembering your content.

This may be the most important meeting of your company's young history. If you don't know your company well enough to sell it, you are not ready for this meeting. Do your homework.

By the way, there is absolutely nothing unprofessional about using notes. The president of the United States uses notes when he reads off his teleprompters. Have a typed outline with some bullets to remind you of key concepts or numbers if you need them.

A typical PowerPoint presentation has everything you plan to say written on the screen. There is no reason for a potential investor to read along as you read.

The VCs you talk to know how to read. Nothing is more patronizing than having someone read something out loud while you are reading to yourself. Presented this way, your graphics literally create a competition between you and the screen onto which you have projected your presentation. No matter how brilliant you or your slides are, either you or your presentation graphics is going to lose that competition.

If you have determined that having a VC read about your company is the best way for you to get your capital, then just send it to them and let them skim it at their leisure. This way the VC can look at all 40 slides at once and dismiss your company without ever having to meet with you. Sure saves time!

Lousy Reason 4: People remember more when they see and hear than when they just hear.

Absolutely true. And if you were trying to help these people pass an exam, showing them slides might help them take better notes so that they could take them home and study them. Better still, e-mail them your text slides and give them an exam on your company when you get there for your first meeting! Remember, this process is not about education. It is about connecting and moving others to action.

Strategically, it does not matter whether they remember a single word of what you have said. If the other person in that meeting is willing to do what you want them to do at the end, you have been successful. If they remember what your company and product does, but they are unwilling to take the next step, you have failed. At any given point in a meeting, you should be less worried about retention than about how well they are on track with you. Are the VCs with you in this moment? Are they willing to move with you to the next point? If your visuals are genuinely the best way of creating and maintaining connection and momentum, then they are useful. Otherwise they are in your way.

PowerPoint Is Not a Crime.

Now that you are scared the about using PowerPoint (or maybe just mad as hell), let's talk about how graphics in general can be used to add value.

When should you use visuals?

When the people in your meeting need or demand them.

Many VCs are now so inured to bad PowerPoint (or whatever the graphics program of choice may be), they have fully accepted it as the industry standard and in fact may demand it. Some will become visibly uncomfortable if you don't start your meeting by booting up your laptop. Some will request that you send your "presentation" for review prior to the meeting. Since "The Home Run Hitter's Guide to Fundraising" is built on a foundation of meeting the needs of the investor, refusing to bring a computer to a meeting or to attach a PowerPoint file to an e-mail because this book challenges its value won't help you get your capital. On the other hand, fifteen years of coaching and consulting with highly successful business people – including some of the very VCs you want to speak to – have convinced me that following the herd is a prescription for a long, painful capital-raising campaign.

Just like everyone else in the business world, VCs are victims of the arbitrary escalation of the use of technology in presentation graphics. From an effectiveness standpoint, most of us are worse off using computer graphics than we were when painting animals on cave walls was the technology standard. The bottom line is that the meetings where people just talked to each other worked better then and they still do now. We sized each other up as people. We argued. We jousted, connected or failed to connect. We invested, or chose not to, but did so in the context in which businesses operate – human contact. Our ability to differentiate our capabilities as leaders and thinkers was never greater than when we had to rely solely on who we were and what we knew.

Using Graphic Supporting Tools Effectively

Before PowerPoint and other graphics programs, we had to give great thought to the use of visual support material because they required a special talent and were expensive to develop and deploy. Visual aids were developed as a last resort based on some barrier presented by a concept or idea. "This will take forever to explain" or "they really have to see this to understand it" drove the thinking behind the use and development of the support tools. In the good old days, a picture really was worth a thousand words.

Many of us still labor under the delusion that a presentation developed in PowerPoint is somehow more efficient and concise. With strategic thought and planning, they could be. As they are typically used in boardrooms and in e-mails across the country right now, they are a monumental waste of time and energy. See How PowerPoint Ruined The US Economy on my Web site at:
dansappassociates.com/pdf-files/how-ppt-ruined.pdf

Ask yourself the following questions to make sure you are using those tools in the right way and for the right reasons.

1. Graphic Support Tools: Yes or no?

Do you use visuals or not? You do have a choice. Arriving at your next VC meeting without a laptop does not mean you will be considered unprepared. The context of a meeting sometimes drives the decision for you. Many of the most meaningful business meetings, VC pitches and otherwise, happen in restaurants, taxicabs and hallways. Even though people may try, spontaneous meetings in hallways and taxicabs are not great places for PowerPoint. The type of relationship you have with the VC and the quality of the introduction that got you the meeting can also impact your willingness to "just talk." But especially in small, intimate, early meetings, your willingness to use as little support as possible can speak volumes about your presence and leadership. You simply don't see confident, senior leaders relying on computer-generated graphics to make connections and neither should you.

If you know the VC is absolutely addicted to PowerPoint, you don't want to confound their expectations and take them out of their comfort zone on principle alone. However, if you are radically driven by the needs of the other people in the meeting and you evaluate the ideas you have selected to share from their perspective, you will be in a good position to evaluate whether to use visuals or not.

2. What Type?

What kinds of tools am I talking about here? Just to stimulate your imagination, here is a list of media that can be put to good use during the course of an effective business meeting. The list is limited only by logistics and your imagination. I know an investment bank that had their senior bankers dress in tie-dyed t-shirts and do a can-can in order to make a connection with a very young management team preparing to take their company public. It worked, and the bank was chosen as lead underwriter.

- A cocktail napkin, back of a business card (great pitches happen in bars, restaurants, taxis...)
- A taste or sample
- A photograph
- A flip chart
- A 35mm slide projection
- A PowerPoint slide
- Your product
- An audio clip

- A live action film
- An animation
- A newspaper clipping or magazine article
- A customer or testimonial
- A relaxation and visualization led by the presenting executive

PowerPoint and its computer-generated brethren are not the only games in town. Remember that part of the challenge in your meeting with VCs is creating sophisticated, value-added differentiation. It is extremely difficult to get real differentiation from the same pre-loaded graphics program driving each of your competitor's presentations, no matter how well you use it.

3. What Purpose?

As a strategic resource, visual support tools must solve a problem for the people in your meetings or they will become part of the problem.

If the conversation you are planning with a VC is going to be truly strategic, you must use the same litmus test for developing and using visuals that you used for developing the message and the supporting ideas for the meeting itself: "What must my listener experience, right now, to be more able or wiling to go with me and do my *Result*?" If the answer is "something more than words," then you have the right agenda to develop a graphic tool.

Some VC-focused reasons to use a non-verbal tool:

Clarity and simplicity:
Sometimes the ideas you want to share are so complex that words alone cannot explain them. When you look at your content outline,

put a check mark next to the ones that might be difficult to understand from the perspective of an uninformed outsider. If words alone can't make critical ideas crystal clear and A-B-C simple, then this is probably a good place for some sort of graphic support.

Making the abstract real*:
Some of the ideas you need to share may be highly conceptual and obtuse until you can actually see what it looks like or how it works. When the conceptual nature of an idea is a real impediment for the VC to overcome some cognitive hurdle, then some visual support is appropriate.

* Caveat: A demo of how a product works is not the same thing as a visual representation of the value of the solution to an investor.

Creating a mood:
In most meetings, you won't have the time nor will the VC have the patience for this. But in a public forum, you may want to evoke certain emotions in order to get the audience moving in the desired direction. Fundraisers and politicians frequently use visual tools for this purpose. A photograph of a starving child not only reinforces the facts, but also creates an emotional response. University fundraisers often show a montage of their campus in a way that evokes nostalgia for a potential donor.

Overcome language barriers:
Sometimes language – national, regional, industry and intra-company – can present such a hurdle that a visual representation is the fastest, most effective way to a meeting of the minds.

Reinforcement:

In many meetings, a few key ideas must stand out from the rest in order for an investor to draw the necessary conclusions. These ideas may need some sort of non-verbal support. Reinforcement can, however, be a real Pandora's box. Sometimes an entrepreneur falls in love with every idea he plans to share and concludes that every idea must be reinforced visually, which is now the industry standard – a PowerPoint slide for every idea. When everything is at the same level of importance for your VCs, nothing seems particularly important. Close up, a blade of grass is a singular miracle of nature. From six feet up, a freshly mown lawn is just green. When you try to reinforce everything, you end up reinforcing nothing.

4. Which *ideas* need support?

Once you have decided whether or not you will use some kind of visual support tool and you know why, only now is it time to identify which ideas need some sort of support.

Quite simply, you must go back to your *Result*, your VC *needs* assessment and, of critical importance here, your assessment of your own *needs*. If an idea represents a real hurdle for that VC to move towards your *result* and you can only overcome that hurdle visually, then you must use some sort of graphic support for that idea. Make sure you check your own *needs* at the door, because the habits of even some of the most educated entrepreneurs are to show a visual at every opportunity.

Visual Result

You have a strategic process for identifying whether, where, and why you might use a supporting tool. Now you must ask the strategic question, "How do I want the VC to respond when they see it?" I call this your Visual Result.

A *Visual Result* is the specific conclusion the VC must draw after seeing this visual or graphic. For instance, when your VC sees this visual, they will believe that the Total Available Market is $40 billion for your product or service, or it will be clear how gene matching using an electric connection is more efficient than using gas spectrometry. Your visual provides reinforcement or clarification.

Headlines

Your next challenge is to articulate your *Visual Result* as a headline instead of a title. For instance, "4th Quarter Profits," "Revenue Model" and "Leadership Team" tell us what is on the slide, but not what is important, relevant or compelling about the information.

A more strategic method is to leverage the power of headlines. A good newspaper headline tells the heart of the story in a few well-chosen words and draws explicit conclusions for the people reading them: "US says enemy fire brought down helicopter in Iraq." You almost don't need to read the article because you have the gist of it in the headline. If you see a billboard that says, "Taste great, less filling" and you see two cans of light beer from Miller, you have the whole story. In fact, billboards are another great metaphor for how to develop powerful, useful, graphic support tools.

You don't want your VC reading your content from your slides – you want them listening and responding and hanging on to your every word. A good headline in a presentation graphic articulates a conclusion for the person on the receiving end of the presentation and makes designing the supporting graphic much simpler and more effective. Your headline tells that VC exactly what you want them to know in a few words, with impact.

A title that says "Four-Year Financial Projections" forces the VC to scrutinize the data for a conclusion. A headline that says "Year 4 Profits Top $100M" over a visual of an almost vertical profit line in your graph prompts your VC to wonder, "How are they going to pull that off?" – which is exactly what you want them to ask. Sometimes you don't even need to print your headline in the visual. Some of the most compelling headlines are spoken.

You don't have to be an advertising expert to develop good headlines. Just ask yourself, "What specific conclusion (time, volume, revenue, profits, market penetration, etc.) do I want the person I am speaking with to draw?"

Before you start drawing or creating bar charts, do the following exercise to create an effective headline for each of the graphic support tools you have identified.

GST Exercise Headline

What is the single result, take away, or conclusion you want the VC to have as a result of seeing this visual? Work to articulate that conclusion in a headline of no more than five or six words. Look at your newspapers for example of headlines and work to make yours equally attention-getting.

Give your visuals a good strong headline and then illustrate them simply. If you can't make it simple – visually or verbally – then you don't really understand it.

The Magic Number

This is what you have all been waiting for – the secret to the right number of slides per minute throughout the meeting. Right? OK. Here is the absolute formula:

As few as you can get away with and as many as the people you are talking to need.

If your business truly warrants capital and you can't get an investor without opening your computer, then you don't know your business well enough to ask for venture capital. On the other hand, when you plan your meeting with a genuine sensitivity to the needs of the VC, and a handful of simple, powerful graphics help your business come alive in a way that words alone couldn't, then visual support is absolutely the right choice.

Cocktail Napkins and Billboards

The best support tools are an organic part of a business meeting. The next time you are in a bar, watch the people who are deep in conversation. You might see one person pull out a pen and draw something on a cocktail napkin in order to illustrate the point being made. This is a great metaphor for the effective use of visual tools. One person recognizes that the other person is having a difficult time understanding a concept, so he draws a picture with whatever he has at his disposal. An attorney friend of mine once defended a rock band against a roadie who produced a pie chart drawn on a cocktail napkin as evidence of an explicit contract of a partnership. Your visuals do not have to be sophisticated to do their job. Use the cocktail napkin metaphor as you are choosing which ideas to support and you will probably be OK.

Developing effective, simple visuals is a much greater creative challenge than doing a visual Data Dump. Advertising agencies are paid millions to keep it simple and make it work. The advertising world gives you another powerful metaphor as you begin to design your visuals. Imagine that the people in your meeting are in a car on the freeway driving at 75 mph. Every now and then the car passes a billboard. If that billboard is well designed, everyone in the car draws the same conclusion because of the powerful, pithy headline. The graphic element then instantly illustrates that conclusion. All of that has to happen quickly enough to have impact without causing a pile up on the freeway. Make your visuals into billboards and they will have impact without wrecking the connection.

Chapter

6 Managing the Game: Facilitating a Successful Meeting

The *Ideas* side of the Communication Delta Model triangle is now complete. But before we start working on using your body and voice for maximum impact, it is important to look at the types of situations you are most likely to be in when you meet with a VC.

Most of the time, you will be meeting in the relatively informal confines of an office or conference room. Usually you will go to them; sometimes they may come to you.

The Meeting: Facilitating an Important Conversation

Hopefully, the vast majority of the interactions you have with potential investors starts in either their office or yours. The more contact you have with these folks, the better your chances are. "The Home Run Hitter's Guide to Fundraising" planning process is based on the assumption that you are planning an important conversation, not a formal speech, but it works even if it is a conversation with 1,000 people.

You won't get your capital until you get a VC into an office. Just about everyone who raises VC funds needs to be able to make these intimate meetings work.

Make it Conversational

Most of the time, you won't say exactly what you have planned to say in the exact order you planned to say it. Once you have a few of these small meetings under your belt, you will realize how fluid and truly conversational they are. In fact, a sure sign that the people on the VC side of the table are not engaged, is if they sit silently and wait for you to finish your presentation. If the time you have with a potential investor feels like a presentation, you have left money on the table.

I urge you to think of yourself as a facilitator in these meetings. A facilitator's role is to manage the process of a meeting in a way that leads to an identified *Result*. You have responsibility not only for the process (the way the meeting works) but also the content (what gets said).

Part of your job as the meeting facilitator is to create the experience of a valuable, purposeful conversation. Valuable because the VC should, very early on, understand the opportunity represented by a deepening relationship with you and your company. Purposeful because everything you do and say is part of the process of closing the gap between the *needs* and *interests* of a potential investor and the *result* you want from that meeting. It is a vibrant exchange of value and opportunity.

Facilitation Tips for the VC Meeting

1. **Don't waste their time.**
   We know these folks are busy. If you spend 15 minutes of your half hour talking about the baseball playoffs, don't expect them to give you more time to sell them on your business. Once the relationship is underway, you have plenty of time to talk baseball. This does not mean that you should be brusque or abrupt, but the most

powerful way to engage these people is with a high return opportunity to make their LPs smile.

2. **Don't force your agenda.**
   Once your meeting is underway, you may realize that the needs for this VC are quite different from what you anticipated. If so, the Communication Delta Model gives you a tool for a quick, mental recalibration.

   If that VC is different from what you expected, your initial *Result* may be unachievable and the *Hook* you planned won't work for this individual. Don't panic! Catch your breath, ask the VC what is important to them and test another *Hook* right then and there. With presence and practice, the thinking process behind "The Home Run Hitter's Guide to Fundraising" will become intuitive. Your revised *Result* and *Hook* don't have to be works of art, but they do have to work for your VC. Under pressure (and you will feel pressure, especially in the first few VC meetings), you are likely to retreat to behaviors that are safe and comfortable to you. Sticking to your script no matter what, may make you feel more comfortable (*your need*) but it may well build a wall between you and your capital.

A client of mine in the insurance business used to take pride in the fact that he would glibly start each presentation by telling his prospect that they could ask questions, but if answering took him off track he would have to start the whole thing over again! He thought it was kind of funny. I thought it was funny too, but I also realized he wasn't kid-

ding and that he had so memorized the content that it had virtually lost meaning for him. If it didn't seem to have meaning for him, I guarantee it didn't have meaning for his potential clients.

3. **Check the process with probing questions.**
   If you are not sure your approach is connecting with your VC, just ask them. Have the courage to express your perception of their reaction. For instance: "I can't tell whether this is interesting to you or not. Is there a part of this that doesn't make sense or that you disagree with?" or "It looks like there is something that you aren't quite sure about. Is there something you disagree with?" You don't have to apologize to check in. Delivered well, these process checks can help you look more confident and in charge. Without these probes, it is difficult to know how you are doing. Most VCs won't start nodding their heads like a bobble-head doll even if they really love your business. The more you lead these meetings in a way that creates efficiency and value for the VC, the more you seem like a leader. Nothing says you are a leader like leading.

   Caveat: Some VCs are in such a hurry and are so jaded by lousy presentations, that they will force "bad process" on the meeting. They will demand to see your PowerPoint while you talk and they will summarily dismiss any attempts on your part to facilitate the meeting. When you run into this brand of VC, stay the course defined by this book. Even if you can't see it, these folks with seemingly impenetrable blank stares are responding to the choices you make. Due to the frog-kissing nature of their business, many VCs use a completely neutral physical posture as a defense against getting warts. It simply takes too much energy to become physically involved in all 12 of the presentations they will see that day. Don't let their habits drive yours. If you feel real antipathy with a potential investor, your chances of deepening that relationship are small and possibly ill-advised. You may have to kiss some frogs too. The good news is that good VCs are in the pond as well.

4. **Overcome objections.**
   I have a friend and business associate who now directs a very progressive business incubator but who cut her teeth in business as the CEO of a successful technology startup. This was a good company that raised millions in venture capital and turned that capital into lots more when it was acquired at a healthy multiple. It took her 75 meetings with VCs to get the capital she needed to grow her business.

   You may have to overcome all kinds of hurdles in seeking VC funding. Some are hurdles that you have to deal with by looking for another investment partner. Some are hurdles you can work to overcome in the course of a meeting.

In these meetings, you will face challenges, questions, doubts and even disbelief. While you don't have control over how a VC responds to your ideas and projections, you do have control over how you deal with their responses. When challenged, most people respond in some pretty unconscious ways. This is especially true when we are under the kind of stress associated with a meeting with a VC. For instance, common responses may be:

- *Defensive* – "You don't know what you are talking about! Our research is unassailable!"
- *Fearful* – "Well...maybe you are right. You probably know more about this than I do."
- *Analytical* – "Gartner's research suggests these numbers are accurate."
- *Passive resignation* – No response, moving on to the next bullet point in the outline.

All of these responses leave opportunity on the table. If you don't explore them, you can't find out whether these objections are personal bias, actual experience with a similar product, idle intellectual jousting, or a deal breaker. These response patterns will not help you move the process of this meeting toward the result you want.

<u>Embrace resistance and objections as an opportunity to deepen your understanding of the investor's perspective, thereby deepening the connection.</u> At the same time you can use these bumps in the road as a measuring stick for gauging the distance between where the VC is now and the result you want. You "gauge and advance" by interpreting these objections with probing questions and testing out closes. For instance:

> VC: Your market size seems way out of whack to me. Where did you get these numbers?

You: (***probing question***) I am pretty confident about the quality of the number, but is your concern that the market is not big enough or that we missed something in the research?

VC: No, I know the opportunity is there, but I am curious about the methodology you used to assess your opportunity. Is this bottom-up, top-down, or what?

You: (***closing question***) If you were comfortable that we could capture the number we are proposing here, would this be more interesting as a potential investment?

VC: If you can convince me that you can get that number, you would definitely whet my appetite.

You: (***testing close***) Our research is complex and deep and it may take more time than we have scheduled to put it through the fine tooth comb. Can we carve out some more time today or should we schedule more time on another day?

Even if you are only four minutes into the meeting you have discovered an objection that has allowed you to better understand the needs of this investor. If having them agree to another meeting or begin some initial diligence on your company was the *Result* you wanted, then you have arrived sooner rather than later.

5. **Listen for closing opportunities.**
   Gauging, deepening, and closing around challenges and objections keeps a meeting moving, but it is also critically important to know how and when to bring a meeting to a *Result*. Remember that this meeting is one step in the development of an important business relationship. Keep your Result in the front of your mind, not hidden behind your content. You don't get extra credit for saying everything you had planned to say. Your only payoff comes when the other people in your meeting agree to do the action in the *Result* you have identified.

   When you sense excitement and real interest in moving forward, have the courage to check in with that VC and see if they are ready. I can't tell you the number of opportunities that have been lost because an entrepreneur over-talked an idea. <u>Sales are lost everyday because the "script" didn't request a call to action until the end.</u> You don't have to be a used car salesman to close someone. If you can't close these folks when it is time, you will never get your capital. Many times, the only way you know it is the right time is by asking.

   Smart investors would rather have a hard-driving businessperson at the helm of a portfolio company who happens to know product development than a technology wizard who decided to try to build a business around a product. Investors tell me that leadership is by far the most important intangible in their evaluation of early stage companies. Without real leadership, even mature Fortune 100 companies flounder and fail. Leaders move the people around them to action.

Facilitating your VC meeting to a result requires leadership. I would rather have you go down swinging for a close – and so would smart investors – than have you politely thank them for their time.

6. **Create visuals on the fly.**
   Sometimes creating visuals as you go is the best way to go. I am not suggesting you shouldn't prepare, just that you let your support tools materialize organically – when the VC needs them – in the course of the meeting. Practice drawing your visuals on a dry erase board or flip chart paper. You don't want to do anything for the first time under pressure, so get good at creating your graphics on the fly. This is also a wonderful place to invite the VC to get out of his chair and add to, subtract from, or change your visual in a way that allows them to collaborate, challenge, and engage in a very different way.

7. **Collaborate.**
   Don't underestimate the value of having a smart, seasoned business person focused on you and your business. Your relationship with a good VC will be collaborative. This means that during your meeting, your VC will probably challenge you to change certain aspects of your business plan or product in ways that can make the difference between success and failure. Explore those possibilities and use testing closes around those issues – "If the business plan included this revision, would you be more likely to invest?" Even if a particular VC doesn't invest, you can still get tremendous value from the meeting.

Managing Q&As

In a meeting at a VC's office, you will be lucky to go 30 seconds without interruption and questions. Believe it or not, that is a good thing. You should be concerned if a VC lets you talk uninterrupted for ten minutes at a time. It probably indicates that they are either lost or disinterested. So questions should be an expected part of the give and take in the VC's office, but Q&As in a public forum is a bigger challenge for many entrepreneurs.

Some entrepreneurs are terrified of Q&As because anyone can ask just about anything they want. Others love Q&As because it feels less like a presentation and more like a conversation. Happily, the Communication Delta Model also contains the seeds for successful Q&As. With your *Result* in mind and your *Hook* at the ready, you are in a tremendous position to get your core message out there and begin reinforcing your promise. For those of you who find Q&As challenging, trust that the more practice you have transforming presentations into conversations, the more you will look forward to the final minutes of your talk so you can jump in and start deepening connections with Q&As.

Q&A: A Five Step Method

Before you can apply this simple method, you must be clear about your *Hook* or core value proposition for this audience. Media coaches often help executives develop several "messages" that basically lead back to the same place but keep an executive from sounding either like a one-trick pony or a broken record. If you want to try to sell more than one message in your Q&As, make sure they are all congruent with your *Hook* and the result you want for this talk. If not, you will probably get lots of follow-on questions you don't want to answer.

Once you know the *ideas* you want to try to get to in your answers, the following process can help you get there.

1. **Listen silently and breathe.** In conversation most of us aren't really listening. We are thinking – hard and fast – about what we are going to say next. When we are thinking of our response, we are not fully hearing the question. As a result, we are missing valuable insights into how to connect and how to get to our messages out there. Listening without speaking while we breathe to release tension, puts us in a powerful state of readiness to answer in a way that creates value both for you and the person asking the question.
2. **Pause.** You will learn more about the power of silence in the section on Physical Strategy, but for now simply practice putting some silence between the end of the question and the beginning of your answer. A purposeful pause gives you time to think and validates the quality of the question better than the rote expressions like "great question." You are not in a position to suggest one question is good or bad. Use a moment of silence to evaluate the question first, and then in silence, develop your response.
3. **Evaluate** in silence whether it is a question that can be answered as is or if it is one that:
   - ***needs* clarification** – "Let me make sure I understand what you are asking here."

- ***needs* reframing** because it contains a false premise – "Your question assumes the market for wireless devices has peaked and our research shows we are at the very beginning of the maturity curve. So I can't really answer the question the way you've asked it, but our market research suggests..."
- **shouldn't be answered** for competitive or legal reasons "I can't answer that because this really is our secret recipe, but I can tell you..."
- **you don't want to answer** because you would be required to have a crystal ball to know the answer, or
- **you don't know the answer** – "I don't know the answer to that; I will have to find out. Give me your card and I will research it and get back with you."

Once you know what kind of question you have fielded, you are comfortable that you can and should answer, and you have the answer (all in silence...with practice this will take a second or two), then it is time to compose your response and...

4. **Answer directly and concisely.** "Yes, we are on schedule for a hard launch on Monday," or "325,000 so far," or "All of our developers are in Sri Lanka." This will then give you an opportunity to ...
5. **Bridge to your message.** "This is not something we are simply hoping to do. Our investors will see things happen quickly." Or "...At that volume, we are cash flow positive. In four months we will ramp to ¾ of a million and be profitable," or "In this way we maintain better than six sigma quality at a 40% reduction in HR costs compared to our next nearest competitor and create an even bigger hurdle for new competitors jumping into this space."

With practice, this process becomes absolutely second nature. Watch politicians as both masters and hacks of the trade. It is a core competency for anyone who frequently deals with the media to be able to generate a print-worthy quote or sound bite on the fly. Masters are always quoted on the issues they are trying to sell; hacks just sound like they are trying to sell.

The Suspension of Disbelief

As the leader of a young company looking for capital, your job in an investor meeting is to move someone from one state of being to another. Until the relationship has deepened and both parties are ready for a marriage proposal, your job is to identify what you want for a next date and what that VC needs to hear to be willing to say "yes." They don't have to know everything about you or your company to make a second date. In fact, everything would be an overload and a barrier to moving forward in most cases.

At every stage in the relationship, however, an investor does have to change from thinking "probably not" to thinking "maybe so." In fiction, accepting an improbable reality is called the "suspension of disbelief." The reader doesn't have to believe in order to engage with a story, they just have to not disbelieve. While your company is not fiction, the probability of a significant return may be hard to believe early on. In the early stages of this relationship, you need to close for the "suspension of disbelief." The Communication Delta Model can help you move a VC all the way from disbelief to writing a check, but it has to be accomplished one step at a time.

Chapter 7

The Swing: Delivery for Impact and Influence

Like it or not, most of your ability to have impact and create change in other people comes not from what you say but how you say it. We are hard-wired and conditioned to respond to some people and not to others. We make very quick and often intractable judgments about the people we meet. Understanding the human tendency to judge as you develop your own ability to control the impression you make, gives you extraordinary power to influence the people you talk to.

While it is impossible to get the skill you need from a short book on the physical side of communication effectiveness, you do have to make sure that everything about the impression you make physically is as compelling and strategic as your ideas. What follows are a handful of tips and choices to consider. If you want help mastering this side of the equation you can learn about coaching, seminars and workshops at www.dansappassociates.com. With the right training and practice, every time you talk becomes an opportunity to drive your company forward.

A Strategic Framework

Impact: The Impression of Greatness

I have spoken with hundreds of groups and thousands of individuals about the idea of a physical goal, and the similarity and consistency of the impressions we all want attributed to us is compelling. While it may vary somewhat from culture to culture, by and large we all want the same things said about us, and most of us have a highly consistent yardstick for measuring what it takes to really engage people. It doesn't mean that we have to like them or agree with them, but people who engage us share certain characteristics.

At this point, we are not talking about how you feel; we are only talking about how you look and sound to other people.

For the most part, this is how most of us want to be seen.

Smart	Organized	Intelligent
Knowledgeable	Professional	Personal
Interesting	Real	Charming
Confident	Energetic	Amusing
In Control	Passionate	Like a leader
Impressive	Focused	Engaging

I have further refined this list to a handful of critical characteristics that must be present if you are going to have influence and impact.

The Essence of Impact:

A few common characteristics must be present to make a real impact on your listeners.

Real

You don't have to be Tony Robbins, Tom Peters, or Zig Ziggler to hold people's attention. Do you have habits you need to change in order to connect and have influence? Probably. Does that mean you can't be completely who you are? Absolutely not. In fact, no matter how dazzling your business plan, how large your market, or how proven your team, the VC you are meeting has heard it, seen it and challenged it before. The only real differentiation you have is who you are. This is why the physical side of "The Home Run Hitter's Guide to Fundraising" and the Communication Delta Model is so strategically important.

Yes, you have to be real. But you can't just say "Hey, this is me" and hope for the best. You have to make the choices that allow you to put your best foot forward and maximize your capabilities every time you talk. If you are not willing to experiment with your habits and your physical comfort zone, I promise that once again, you are leaving money on the table.

Do you have to change your personality? Only if it doesn't allow you to make the most of who you are. From years of study and experience in clinical psychology, coaching and consulting, I can tell you that what we describe as our personality is the progressive shaping of certain tendencies, reinforced with years of repetition until they become habits. What were affectations as children become our personalities as adults and annoying quirks as old folks. If your personality keeps you from connecting, then you may have to work on the expression of your personality if you are going to get what you want as a business communicator.

NOTE If you aren't willing to change your behavior, the habits that got you where you are will keep you where you are.

Strength

At your best with a VC, you must appear to have the right to be in that meeting and the right to say what you are saying. You must seem comfortable taking up all of the time and space you need, and you must seem completely comfortable in your own skin. The people in your meetings must experience your strength regardless of your age, experience, the situation, or even how you feel in the moment.

You don't have to seem aggressive or pushy or rude to express your strength. In fact you had better not. But you certainly cannot seem to be asking for permission.

- A strong body is balanced, solid, forward, open and relaxed.
- A strong voice is clear and audible but never shouted and never in hurry.
- Experienced, strong leaders take their time and are comfortable with silence.

Other words often associated with strength include expressions of power, confidence, authority, and control. But you can't afford to wait to feel your strength before you express it.

Passion

Strength is the cornerstone of leadership, but without an expression of passion, strength can seem distant, matter-of-fact or even wooden. Every entrepreneur I have ever worked with swore to their complete and utter commitment and passion for their company. But it is not enough for you to feel passionate. If you are going to have real impact, the people around you must experience your passion. The people you talk to will feel secure in your strength, but will only be drawn in by the expression of your passion.

An expression of your real passion is not the same thing as enthusiasm. Enthusiasm may seem unfocused and often seems false and fleeting. Cheerleaders express smiling enthusiasm and the stereotypical used car salesmen express the oily variety.

Your passion must seem to be an expression of your real commitment to your company and to the words you say. You don't have to wave your arms and jump up and down, but if you are not physically involved, others may question your passion.

It requires tremendous energy for a VC to listen to yet another pitch. It is your job to create that energy with the expression of your passion.

- A passionate body leans slightly forward, bent at the waist and leading with the heart.
- Arms and hands help to emphasize important points, but are completely at rest when not purposefully employed.
- When you really care about an idea, you work hard to open your mouth in order to form your words with energy.
- A passionate voice is easy for others to hear. It is not the VC's job to work hard to hear you.
- Silence can often create a sense of commitment better than any word or sound.

For many executives and for many reasons, expressing what looks like real passion often feels uncomfortable and theatrical. Church, schools, and many work places conspire to make us self-conscious and self-censuring. Especially for young, highly intellectual, and academically oriented business people, what feels like a wild exaggeration of physical energy just begins to look real, comfortable and committed. But you cannot express all of your strength without also expressing tremendous passion, and often what feels comfortably committed seems restrained, cautious and calculating. This is definitely one area where the growing edge will be an uncomfortable place to be for a while.

You risk more in seeming disinterested than in seeming too interested. You are better off having someone complain about your obvious passion than your obvious boredom or exhaustion.

Connection

Part of what makes the Communication Delta Model unique is that it explores empathy as a tool for driving business results. Empathy is making yourself available to other people and responsive to their needs. When you choose to empathize, you make yourself vulnerable and as a result you are open to a deeper connection. All of the choices – intellectual, strategic and physical – in this process bring you to a stronger connection to the people you are talking to. And yet there are a few key choices you have to make if you are really going to connect.

You won't connect by simply making eye contact. Eye contact is a technique they teach in public speaking 101. Some folks would have you believe that looking at the clock on the back wall or sweeping your eyes from one side of the room to the other creates the illusion of connection. The truth is speakers who practice making this kind of "eye contact" either look like they can't wait for their time to be up or like they are a spectator at a tennis match. You are either genuinely seeing people or not. No, you won't make an effective connection by staring unblinkingly at your VC, but an unwillingness to see and be seen can seem shifty, fearful or deferential. While the issue may be less dramatic in a small room with one or two people, your willingness to see and be seen may be the single most important thing you can say about your leadership.

- A connecting communicator finishes an entire thought with someone before pausing and moving on to someone else.
- A connecting communicator literally reaches out with hands, arms, and torso to get with the other people in a meeting.
- Everything about a connecting communicator says "Are you getting this? What more do you need?"
- A connecting communicator works to understand the words, gestures, and posture of the other people to deepen and maintain a connection.
- Connecting communicators know that they must be vulnerable to the reaction of the people in their meetings or they leave opportunity behind.

A connection is not something you do to the people you are talking to; connecting is something that happens to you. The real power to influence as a communicator is in how available and comfortably vulnerable you can allow yourself to be. Remember, your audience's reactions and responses to you and your ideas determine your success.

Vulnerability is a fundamentally human condition. Our skin is soft and mostly hairless, we don't have sharp claws and teeth, and we couldn't outrun or outfight a mountain lion, literally, to save our lives. Ironically, the more we create an impression that suggests we are comfortable with that vulnerability, the less vulnerable we seem. A solid, neutral stance – relaxed, open, and vulnerable, sends the message that "I am OK. I am comfortable making myself a big target. I can take it and I don't need to protect myself."

The leaders whose presence has changed history most – Jesus, Buddha, Gandhi, etc. — understood that their willingness to embrace their human vulnerability vastly increased their power and influence. The welcoming postures that characterize photographs, paintings and idealized characterizations suggest complete transparency and vulnerability. They had impact partly because they were vulnerable: completely authentic, trustworthy, confident, and at peace.

Luckily, you don't have to be a deity or completely enlightened to learn this lesson: The less you seem defended, the less you seem to need defending.

Your Voice

Of course, you can't just sit there, beatifically, in silence and expect a VC to invest in your company. If you are going to have maximum impact, your voice has to be as compelling as the rest of you. You can make five simple but powerful choices that will make a huge difference in your quest for impact.

1. **Pause:** The silences makes your ideas seem more important and gives you time to think. A rushed, rapid delivery will make you seem less sure of yourself. Take your time and let your audience think about what you just said.

2. **Inhale:** You can't put the strength of your convictions behind your words without breath. In fact, without air in your lungs, you can't create voice at all. Try it. Exhale all of your air and try the preamble to the constitution. See? Can't do it. A bite of air gives you all the breath you need to say most ideas. When you run out – you

guessed it – pause and inhale another bite of air.

3. **Project**: This means you use the inhaled air to "throw" your ideas to your listeners. Don't just let the words fall out, use your whole body to send your ideas with power to your listeners. It helps if you let your torso come forward while you speak and it looks more convincing too. Don't confuse projection with volume. You can amplify an under projected voice and it still seems to lack power. On the other hand, you can share your voice powerfully without it being loud. Projection works in small meetings as well as formal presentations.

4. **Use your mouth (articulation):** When you open your mouth and work hard with your mouth to form your words, you look and sound more committed and convincing. If you don't open your mouth and use your lips, tongue and jaw, you look held back and bored. This takes some practice for lots of people, but it makes a huge difference. Use Jim Carrey as a model for this exercise. Love him or hate him, he seems committed!

5. **Make statements, not questions:** Avoid "up-speak," or ending your thoughts on an upward note as if asking a question. Nothing robs your voice of its strength like up-speak. Practice ending your thoughts on a downward note. Even a question sounds more convincing when it ends on a downward note. Try it: What time is it?⇧ or What time is it?⇩

The Power of Silence

Consciously or unconsciously, many people fear silence more than anything else during communication. Getting comfortable with silence is one of the most powerful tools you have, not only for the impression you make, but also for adding impact to your ideas. Often the person using silence – purposeful pauses – with the most skill and comfort seems to be the most powerful person in the room. Comfort with silence is also universally understood as a critical skill and choice in important business negotiation.

- Pausing gives you time to collect your thoughts. When you pause regularly your ideas seem better organized and more succinct. This is especially important for tough "Q&A" situations.

- A pause gives your listeners time to digest your ideas. Yes, we can hear more quickly than we can talk, but hearing, understanding and impact are different phenomena. Silence creates impact.

- A bit of silence before any idea makes it sound more important because it sounds as if you have given that idea some thought. That's one reason why a quickly read speech will never have the impact of someone really talking with passion.

- Pausing gives you time to exhale and release tension so you feel more relaxed. Then inhale to fuel a well projected voice. The faster you go, the less you breathe, and the less you breathe, the faster you go.

- A speaker who is comfortable with silence looks and sounds confident and in control. It's as if the willingness to pause, breathe and think says to the people you are talking to, "I'm OK up here. I'm not in a hurry and what I'm saying is so important I want you to think about it."

- Consistent, purposeful pauses eliminate distracting verbal fillers. When you break up your thoughts with silences, those fillers go away. In a counterintuitive way, pausing, even pausing badly, helps your ideas seem better organized.

- Pauses punctuate. On the written page, commas, periods, colons, etc., create meaning for the reader. The people listening to you talk use gestures, voice inflection and especially silence to do the same for the spoken word.

Presence and Presentness: Connecting With Others, Connecting With Yourself

Companies often send executives to me to help them develop leadership presence. When I ask what that looks like, I usually get a list of adjectives that probably looks pretty much like the characteristics that help you to have impact as a communicator (see "The Impression of Greatness). I want to challenge your thinking about your presence and in the meantime create an opportunity for a deeper connection with both your VC and yourself.

People sometimes describe media stars, politicians, and royalty as having "presence" as if some mystical aura surrounding them makes them different from normal people. The truth is that these folks are used to being in the spotlight and either through training or the school of hard knocks, they have found a way to keep their best foot forward no matter what. Those with truly astonishing presence find a way to make everyone they contact feel uniquely important in that instant. Bill Clinton, for example, was famous for this ability.

The magical presence these people have is nothing more than making habits out of the choices we have been discussing. The ability to carry yourself with a combination of real authenticity in a world of phonies, with strength in the face of harsh public scrutiny, with passion in light of Herculean schedules and, most importantly the consistent willingness to be vulnerable and available for a real connection, is attractive whether you are a movie star or an entrepreneur. It is also wildly differentiating. It defines star power and a specific kind of presence.

You can develop it, but it requires commitment, patience, and hard work.

The ultimate presence, however, is rarer, harder to come by and much more important for business leaders. This presence connects you not only with others but also deeply and profoundly with the truth of who you really are. I call it *Presentness* and while it is hard to define in a few words it means that wherever you are, whatever you are doing, you are completely there and completely doing that thing.

As an entrepreneur growing a business, it is almost impossible not to get caught up in a thousand things at the same time. When you do, you are living at least as much in the past and the future as you are in the present moment. As a practical matter, you will not respond as effectively to a VC's questions if you are thinking about next month's payroll or last month's missed deadlines. In business, as in life, the only reality is the present. This doesn't mean you can't plan. It means that when you plan, you plan with all of your heart, mind and soul right then and there.

Keep asking yourself, *"What is the opportunity/challenge right now? What can I do right now?"* and then do it, now. The past is at best, an inaccurate memory. The future is at best only a maybe. Living in those times wastes your now and makes you crazy.

Now is all you have.

Those few who live in the now make things happen. They look and sound like the people you want to be with. They attract, and they have extraordinary presence, because they are extraordinarily present.

Chapter

8 Pre-Game Jitters: Managing Flight or Flight

The model is complete. Now all you have to do is go out there and execute. Of course it is easier said than done – especially if the idea of meeting with VCs or presenting in a big room full of people is the scariest thing you can think of.

For some of you, the greatest challenge in raising capital is neither planning, nor delivery. It is intestinal fortitude. Some folks would argue that this section should come first in this process, not last. It is here because if you are ready strategically and you have a physical plan of attack, most of you simply won't be as apprehensive. A good plan is better than Pepto-Bismol, especially if you are new to the process of meeting with and talking to the venture community. That said, the better you understand your response to the situations you are about to face, and the more you prepare, the less impact the butterflies in your stomach will have on your ability to get your capital.

Jerry Seinfeld once said that since public speaking is America's number one fear "If invited to a funeral, most Americans would rather be in the coffin than standing at the pulpit delivering the eulogy." No magic formula can ease your nerves, but you can make some powerful choices that will help you feel more comfortable and in control.

Recognize it. Your body is going to respond, so learn your own response pattern and make friends with it. "Heart rate up? Right on time. Sweaty palms? Check. Now here comes the cotton mouth." You do not have to encourage it, but if you do not know your own pattern, you will be surprised, and that will definitely make the cycle worse.

Reality check. Most of us (especially in business) are so concerned about winning and being perfect, we forget why we are communicating in the first place. Developing and deepening a relationship based on mutual value is what you are there for. Closing the deal, winning the contract, getting your capital, can happen only if the people in your meeting engage with the ideas you share. The people on the other side of the table are not the enemy.

Stop and exhale. No, you do not have to repeat a mantra, but when you stop talking and exhale all the air in your lungs you are literally telling your central nervous system that you are not under attack. You do it instinctively when you walk in your front door at the end of a long hard week and say Ahhhhhh. Remember, the silence that feels like an eternity to you, looks and sounds like control and confidence to the others in the room. The pause gives you and other people time to think – you about what you are going to say, everyone else about what you've just said and what you might say next.

Put the adrenaline to work.

Fight or flight isn't there to make you feel nauseated. Fight or flight is meant to help you in challenging or threatening situations. If you do not use your natural physical response for what it is intended, it will make you feel crazy, and probably make you look uncomfortable. How do you use it? Open up! Get your body involved! Project your voice! Let your passion come through! Remember, the more adrenaline you use, the less there is swirling around in your body making you feel nervous. Expressing your passion makes you look more interesting and interested in your ideas. That is what the physical response is for.

Knowing is great, but doing is what makes change. You will not feel more comfortable in your next critical communication unless you practice and make these choices into habits.

Just before the meeting.

I do not recommend that you mentally rehearse content – especially just before a meeting. You should only practice your content in real time, out loud. Practicing content in your head only reinforces too rapid a pace and an overemphasis on getting each word just right. The VC has no idea which words you have chosen to share or in what order. Your meeting need not, should not, and will not be word-for-word as you have practiced it. If it is, you have left out the people you came to meet. The best meetings develop and deepen professional relationships. You do not get credit for having said exactly what you had planned to say.

Do, however, visualize the physical choices you are working on making into habits. The power of the relationship between these choices, your comfort, and your ability to think on your feet cannot be overemphasized. If you focus on the words and forget one in the meeting, everything will swell into the flight or fight vortex. Focus on your body and the thoughts will come.

Chapter

9 Your Turn at Bat: Swing for the Fence

If you have worked through this process, you are better prepared than 90% of the entrepreneurs talking to the same VC on any particular day. I hope this process helps you get what you need to grow your business.

Bucking the current industry standards by using the Communication Delta Model is a powerful source of differentiation and even a competitive advantage. There is risk, however, in not following the herd. You run the risk of standing out, the risk of seeming original, of being your own person. And, as you communicate with empathy and purpose, you run the very real risk of developing and deepening important relationships. Some of those relationships will help your business succeed; some will merely help you live a fuller life.

Take the risk to communicate strategically, not habitually. Let the best of who you can be and the value of your company differentiate you from the dozens of rote PowerPoint presentations that investor will see that day. Stay in the moment, work to connect, and let the power of the "The Home Run Hitter's Guide to Fundraising" and the Communication Delta Model help you take the next big step in allowing your leadership to make your company the huge success you know it can be.

I wish you good fortune and much success!

About the Author

Dan Sapp has over 15 years experience consulting and coaching with performance driven individuals and teams. In 1997 Sapp founded Dan Sapp & Associates (DSA) and gained a reputation for his ability to help executives brand their leadership through their impact as communicators. DSA has helped countless early stage and mature companies raise capital through both the private and public markets. Dan has lectured at UC Berkeley's Haas Business School's executive education program, at Duke's Fuqua School of Business and currently consults with the Dean and the development team at Stanford's Graduate School of Business. Sapp's clients have included senior executives, partners and leadership teams from Silicon Valley Bank, Nokia, Hellman & Friedman LLC, 3i, Ernst & Young, Pillsbury Winthrop Shaw Pitman, Mellon Capital Management, Skyy Spirits and many others.

Following completion of his graduate studies in clinical psychology, Dan started his management-consulting career with a small organizational development firm based in London.

Before launching his consulting career, with an undergraduate degree in Psychology from UNC at Chapel Hill and his experience as a prep and collegiate athlete, Sapp became a pioneering fitness and conditioning coach. His clients included not only corporate executives, but also competitive age group athletes as well as Olympic gold medalist Bryan Boitano.

He lives with his wife and two sons, their 85lb rescue dog Guinevere and Matilda the cat in Mill Valley, CA.

Create Thought Leadership for your Company

Books deliver instant credibility to the author. Having an MBA or PhD is great, however, putting the word "author" in front of your name is similar to using the letters PHD or MBA. You are no long Michael Green, you are "Author Michael Green."

Books give you a platform to stand on. They help you to:

- Demonstrate your thought leadership
- Generate leads

Books deliver increased revenue, particularly indirect revenue

- A typical consultant will make 3x in indirect revenue for every dollar they make on book sales

Books are better than a business card. They are:

- More powerful than white papers
- An item that makes it to the book shelf vs. the circular file
- The best tschocke you can give at a conference

Why wait to write your book?

Check out other companies that have built credibility by writing and publishing a book through Happy About

Contact Happy About at 408-257-3000 or go to http://happyabout.info.

Other Happy About Books

This book speaks to the starry-eyed young entrepreneur who has big business ideas but no idea of what it takes to have it all, as well as the well-established business leader who has achieved success and now wants to somehow fit a life into those dreams.

Paperback: $19.95 148pgs
eBook: $11.95 150pgs

Is it who or what one knows that makes the difference? Both! 'Tales From The Networking Community' gives you tips, techniques and shares anecdotal stories that will help you succeed with your networking goals.

Paperback: $19.95 80pgs
eBook: $11.95 82pgs

Purchase these books at Happy About http://happyabout.info or at other online and physical bookstores.

LaVergne, TN USA
21 April 2010
180114LV00001B/5/A

9 781600 050596